Country Furniture

TIME-LIFE BOOKS

Alexandria, Virginia

Country Furniture

*America's
rich legacy of design
and craftsmanship*

C O N T E N T S

Simple Country Furnishings

Seating Furniture · Country Tables
Making a Country Bench · Stands and Dry Sinks · Food Storage
The Versatile Hoosier · Country Cupboards
From a Craftsman's Handbook · Bedroom Furniture
Children's Furniture

At Home with Country Furniture

Living History · New and Old
Buying Country Antiques · Painted Charm
Versatile Wicker · A Folding-Chair Slipcover · Shaker Refinement
Purely Regional · Caring for Wood Furniture · Spanish Colonial
Colorful Choices · Well-Worn Patinas
Through the Looking Glass
Suitable Settings

CREDITS

INDEX

ACKNOWLEDGMENTS

American country furniture encompasses an extraordinary range of types made over a time span of several hundred years, and pieces often differ significantly in quality of craftsmanship, place of origin, and appearance. But whether produced by the hands of a farmer, by the workshop of a well-known country craftsman, or even by the factories of an expanding machine age, all country furniture seems to share an inherent character—and often a distinctive quirkiness—that is central to its appeal.

Among the most familiar country furnishings are handsome, utilitarian pieces, such as farm tables and hutches, which were crafted in no particular style and whose makers remain anonymous. Yet many country antiques are quite remarkable and do have recognizable roots. From the 17th century through the early 1800s, American furniture was enormously influenced by European and English styles, which urban cabinetmakers in this country adapted to colonial tastes. In turn, country craftsmen copied urban furniture, modifying it to suit the homes of people who lived on farms and in small villages. Rural householders were eager to keep up with fashion, but were of relatively modest means and tended to be conservative in their preferences. As a result, country furniture was generally simplified. Made of local woods, it often featured painted decoration rather than the costly carving and veneers of high-style pieces produced in furniture-making centers like Newport and Philadelphia.

In addition to showing distinct stylistic influences, country furniture also often displays strong regional characteristics that were determined in large part by the ethnic backgrounds of the people who settled in different areas of the country. The design and decoration of early furniture made in New England, for example, reflect the heritage of colonists who were primarily of English, Scottish, and Irish descent. Furniture makers in the Southwest were strongly affected by the blend of Spanish, Indian, and Anglo-American traditions that dominated the region, while settlers in Pennsylvania produced Germanic designs. The rich mix of cultures that made up America's melting pot during the 18th and 19th centuries was responsible not only for the introduction of new and varied forms to this country, but also for a wealth of expressive decoration.

In the Victorian era, furniture became even more diverse in character as a thirst for novelty produced an unprecedented range of styles. These were made accessible to an increasingly broad market through the technological advances of a new industrialism. At the same time, tastes were dictated by a widespread yearning for an idealized past, when life was believed to be simpler. Only in this Victorian age of romanticism, it seems, could such oddities as furniture made from animal horns or tree stumps find a welcome place in America's parlors. And yet, it is perhaps a similar nostalgia for the "good old days" that makes country furniture so desirable today.

ANATOMY OF FURNITURE

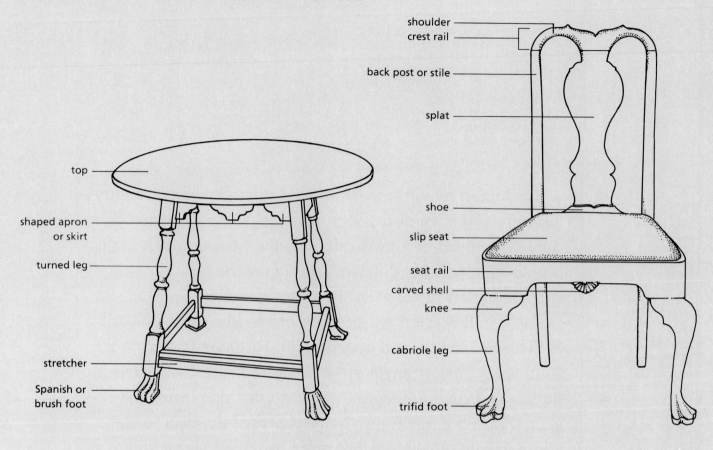

top

shaped apron or skirt

turned leg

stretcher

Spanish or brush foot

shoulder

crest rail

back post or stile

splat

shoe

slip seat

seat rail

carved shell

knee

cabriole leg

trifid foot

cleat

side panel

lid

stile

muntin

split baluster

carved panel

molding

boss or jewel

drawer front

turned pull

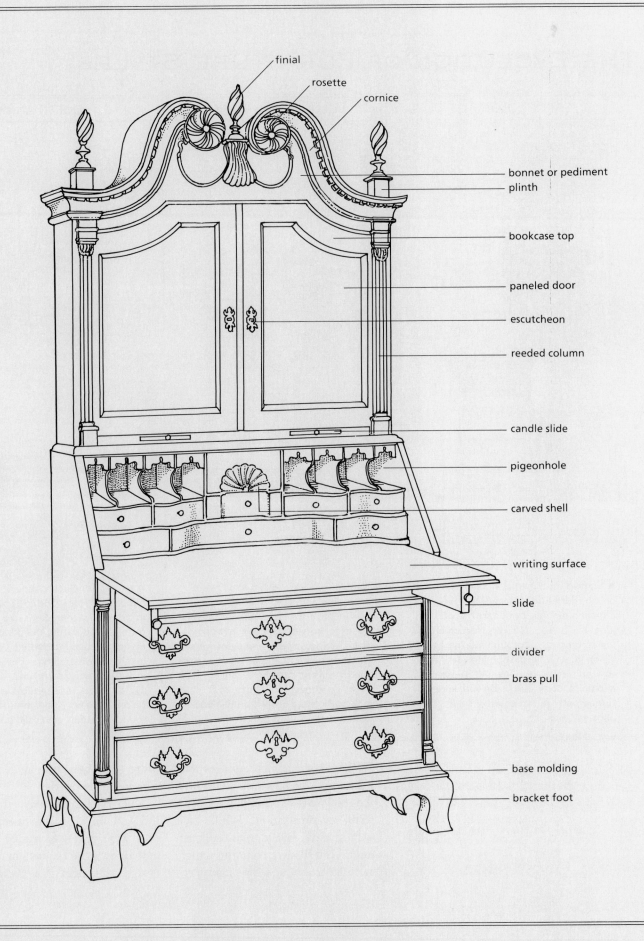

finial

rosette

cornice

bonnet or pediment

plinth

bookcase top

paneled door

escutcheon

reeded column

candle slide

pigeonhole

carved shell

writing surface

slide

divider

brass pull

base molding

bracket foot

THE EVOLUTION OF FURNITURE STYLES

EARLY COLONIAL	WILLIAM AND MARY	QUEEN ANNE
1630 - 1710	1690 - 1730	1725 - 1760

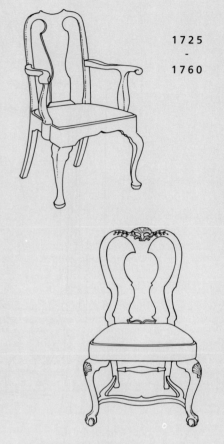

◆ Derived from medieval forms, 17th-century furniture is massive and rectilinear. Common woods are oak and pine. The heavy, solid construction is often accomplished through mortise-and-tenon joinery. Decoration includes flat, stylized carving, applied split balusters, and paint. Chairs are made with lathe-turned posts and spindles, or solid paneled backs.

◆ Named for King William and Queen Mary of England (who ruled together from 1689 to 1694), furniture in this style is noted for curved lines and vertical forms. Carving, veneer, and paint were favored decorations. Chairs typically have turned posts and stretchers, carved "brush" or turned "ball" feet, and leather upholstery or split-spindle backs and rush seats.

◆ Named for Queen Anne of England (who ruled from 1702 to 1714), furniture in this style is characterized by curvaceous forms. It was during this period that mahogany was introduced. Construction involves dovetails and tenons. Decoration includes veneer, paint, and carving. Typical chairs have cabriole legs with carved "pad" or "claw-and-ball" feet, round shoulders, and solid back splats.

The chart above chronicles early American furniture styles from the 1600s to the mid-1800s, using the chair as illustration. While style names vary—what one collector might call Federal, another might call Neoclassical, for instance—those given here are names that are commonly used today.

American furniture styles followed those of England and Europe, and they were generally named for the monarchs who reigned or for the design influences that prevailed at

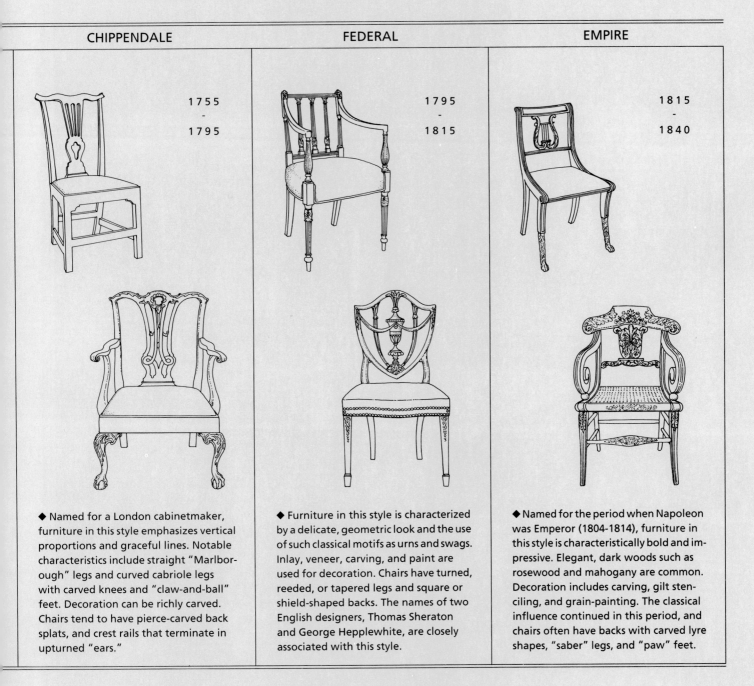

CHIPPENDALE	FEDERAL	EMPIRE

CHIPPENDALE 1755 - 1795

FEDERAL 1795 - 1815

EMPIRE 1815 - 1840

◆ Named for a London cabinetmaker, furniture in this style emphasizes vertical proportions and graceful lines. Notable characteristics include straight "Marlborough" legs and curved cabriole legs with carved knees and "claw-and-ball" feet. Decoration can be richly carved. Chairs tend to have pierce-carved back splats, and crest rails that terminate in upturned "ears."

◆ Furniture in this style is characterized by a delicate, geometric look and the use of such classical motifs as urns and swags. Inlay, veneer, carving, and paint are used for decoration. Chairs have turned, reeded, or tapered legs and square or shield-shaped backs. The names of two English designers, Thomas Sheraton and George Hepplewhite, are closely associated with this style.

◆ Named for the period when Napoleon was Emperor (1804-1814), furniture in this style is characteristically bold and impressive. Elegant, dark woods such as rosewood and mahogany are common. Decoration includes carving, gilt stenciling, and grain-painting. The classical influence continued in this period, and chairs often have backs with carved lyre shapes, "saber" legs, and "paw" feet.

the time that the style was introduced. There was usually a time lag before the style became popular in America.

Because there is overlap from one period to the next, the dates assigned to each style are approximate. Much of America's colonial population lived in rural areas where tradition was important and fashions changed slowly. A new style might be introduced in Newport or Boston at the same time that an old style was still popular in the country.

A History of American Interiors

*a gallery of rooms reveals
a changing concept of "home"*

The following chapter includes museum rooms that are believed to be accurate representations of period interiors from the late 17th century to the early 1800s. These interiors seem sparse by today's standards, but the furnishings and their arrangement reveal much about how people lived.

Well into the 1700s, one room served many needs, and furniture was moved from room to room. As settlers prospered, rooms and furnishings became more specialized, and decorative additions, such as rugs, wallpaper, and framed portraits, were more common. A parlor in the early 1700s typically contained little more than a bed and a chair or two; the same room a century later might boast a carpet, an upholstered furniture suite, and a piano. Because the decor of a room was updated gradually over the years, it was not uncommon for old pieces to be saved and mixed with new acquisitions. Nevertheless, homeowners were proud of their belongings, and chose their furnishings with a fashion-conscious eye.

Simple, utilitarian pieces furnish an early colonial parlor at Historic Deerfield.

EARLY
COLONIAL

The concept of the home in 17th-century America was closely linked to a medieval way of life. Although some colonists were living in houses with six or more rooms by the end of the 1600s, two-room dwellings remained common well into the 1700s. These two rooms—usually called the "hall," or kitchen, and the "parlor"—served many purposes, including cooking, eating, storage, and sleeping. The parlor, however, contained the family's best furniture and master bed, as shown at right.

Few comforts existed, and furnishings were practical by necessity. Blanket chests doubled as seats, and trestle tables were made so that they could be easily dismantled to save space. Generally of oak or pine, early colonial furniture was heavy in form and proportion. It was made by turners—who created the spindles, posts, and legs for chairs—and by joiners, who crafted some of the chairs and also constructed the larger pieces.

This early colonial parlor at Historic Deerfield in Massachusetts contains furnishings that would have been found in the home of a successful middle-class farmer. The pine blanket chest dates from 1694. The stool, chair, and table were made in the early 1700s, but their medieval forms are tied to the 17th century. The candlesticks, mirror, worsted bed hangings, and chamber pot were imported to this country from England and Germany.

EARLY BED DRESSINGS

From the 1600s until the mid-1800s, elaborately draped tall-post beds were found in virtually every American household that could afford them. Even where low-post beds were used, they were commonly enclosed by curtains that hung from a cord attached to the ceiling with hooks or rings.

The practice of enclosing a bed at night to create privacy and keep sleepers warm had existed for centuries in Europe and England before the colonists arrived here. Parlors frequently doubled as bedrooms in early America, and the need for curtained privacy lasted until the revolutionary period, when second-story "chambers" became the only rooms commonly used for sleeping.

The beds that were used in those early parlors were prominently displayed, and it was important that they favorably reflect the economic status of a household. Indeed, they were by far the most elaborate—and complicated—pieces of furniture in a house. Only the mattress was actually known as the bed; the wooden bedstead, whether tall-post or low-post, was called a frame. The hang-

Popular throughout the colonial period, homespun linen was often used for bed "furniture." Simple checked hangings and a scalloped valance dress the 1775 bed above. The wool spread is crewel-embroidered. By 1790, hangings like those at right, made of printed English linen, were the latest fashion.

ings—which typically included a tester or canopy cloth to cover the top of the frame; a headcloth hung against the wall to insulate against cold; head curtains and foot curtains that could be pulled around to enclose the bed; a coverlet; valances; and bases (dust ruffles)—were known as furniture. (This term referred to the job of the upholsterer, who "furnished out" a newly made frame with hangings.)

English style-books that included directions for making bed furniture in the latest fashion were available in 18th-century America. Homeowners often hired a professional upholsterer to furnish their beds, but if necessary, they also made their own hangings. Because the hangings required fifty to sixty yards of fabric, they were by far the most valued and expensive part of the bed.

It was not until the early 19th century—when good air circulation became associated with good health—that the use of curtained beds was discouraged. By the 1830s, the draperies had been reduced in size and weight and were usually added to a bed purely for decorative effect.

The 1815 bed above displays bed hangings in a 19th-century style that eliminated the separate valance and dust ruffle. They are made of roller-printed cotton, newly available at the time. By 1830, bed hangings such as those at left, made of cotton dimity, were used only for decorative effect.

WILLIAM AND MARY
1690-1730

By the William and Mary period, settlers had become well established in the colonies, and home furnishings—no longer limited to necessities—demonstrated a taste for the latest English styles. Furniture of the period became more elegant and baroque in feeling, reflecting the influence that the French and Dutch were then having on English furniture design. Chair backs were elongated and often had crests with scrolled carving; the turnings on chair and table legs became crisper.

The parlor still accommodated a variety of uses, but it was not uncommon to find the walls finished with raised paneling or painted woodwork. A room like the one shown here might contain several chairs and perhaps a gate-leg table. Large "desk and bookcases" appeared for the first time, as did the daybed, which in America was called a couch. Richly carved and made comfortable with a soft "squab," or pillow, the couch provided a fashionable spot to nap. Such furnishings, created for specific purposes, signaled a new sense of luxury.

The William and Mary furnishings in this parlor at the Museum of Early Southern Decorative Arts in Winston-Salem, North Carolina, include a "desk and bookcase" and gate-leg table, c. 1720, and a day bed, c. 1725; all are walnut. The cherry and hickory armchair was made in Virginia, also during the 18th century.

QUEEN ANNE: 1725-1760

As the colonists became more established on their farms and in business during the Queen Anne period, they naturally built larger houses. Room use became more specialized: two-story houses, for example, allowed for bedrooms or "chambers" on the second floor. Although carpets and window curtains were still rarities, the growing prosperity of the colonies was reflected in more conscious decoration. Walls were frequently plastered and whitewashed or—if a family could afford it—wallpapered. Wall paneling was usually painted in colors that coordinated with bed hangings and other fabrics. Small mirrors—imported, costly, and a sign of success—were proudly hung on walls, or used on special dressing tables.

Lighter and more delicate than earlier pieces, furniture in the Queen Anne style had lost its ties with the heavy forms of the 17th century. Surfaces were smooth, with little ornament. The curvaceous cabriole leg, often ending in a pad foot, began to replace the turned leg. Chair backs were made with rounded shoulders and vase-shaped center splats.

These graceful, curving forms reflected the influence of Chinese furniture design. By 1725, England had increased its trade with the East, and English adaptations of China's exotic furniture were quickly in demand among America's fashion-conscious.

As American craftsmen of various heritages copied the English adaptations, regional characteristics developed. Made of mahogany, the North Carolina tall-post bed in the chamber at left, for instance, is believed to have been crafted by a Huguenot settler from the Beaufort County area. Its heavy legs and "hoof" feet were design elements used in France. The three-sided design of the infant bed, which allowed a mother to easily tend her child at night, was used exclusively in the American South.

The furnishings in this bedroom at the Museum of Early Southern Decorative Arts are typical of the stylish pieces that would have been owned by a middle-class merchant or planter during the Queen Anne period. The canopied bed, infant bed, chair, and dressing table were all made in the southern colonies. The crewel-embroidered bed hangings, mirror, candlestick, and chamber pot were imported from England in the mid-1700s.

CHIPPENDALE
1755-1795

By 1760, even furniture makers in small towns in America were making Chippendale furniture, emulating the high-style designs that were then the rage in Philadelphia and Boston. While the basic forms of the earlier Queen Anne style continued in the Chippendale period, the smooth surfaces gave way to rich decorative carving: the more carving, the more expensive the piece. Chairs were designed with delicate pierce-carved back splats, and the finest furniture pieces had claw-and-ball feet.

By this time, the parlor, now known as the best room or "setting parlour," might boast wallpaper and an imported English carpet. As in the parlor at right, rooms were arranged with all the furnishings placed along the walls: desks were set near windows, which provided a natural light source, and tables were pulled into the center of a room only when needed. Once the furniture was returned to the perimeter, a room was considered "straight"—hence the expression "to straighten a room."

The parlor of the Sayward-Wheeler House in York Harbor, Maine, right, is decorated just as it was by its owner, Jonathan Sayward, in 1760. A successful merchant, Sayward chose stylish furnishings to reflect his social status. The mahogany Chippendale chairs were made nearby in Portsmouth, New Hampshire; the tea table is a Boston piece.

THOMAS CHIPPENDALE

The son of a furniture joiner, Thomas Chippendale was born in England in 1718. He was trained as a master carver and cabinetmaker, and already had a following of patrons when he opened a furniture and upholstery shop in London in 1755.

By that date, Chippendale's name was also known in America: in 1754 he had published a lavishly illustrated style book, *The Gentleman and Cabinet-Maker's Director,* and copies were circulating among makers of high-style furniture in this country. Subsequent editions of the book, with additional designs "suited to the fancy and circumstances of persons in all degrees of life," appeared in 1755 and 1762, and they helped make the author the most widely known English cabinetmaker of his time.

Many of Chippendale's designs called for mahogany, which was imported to Europe and America from the West Indies. The fine grain of the wood allowed for the elaborate and fragile carving he developed in "the Gothic, Chinese, and modern taste" and used liberally on pierce-carved fretwork and on table legs.

In America, such delicate, formal furniture was generally considered overly fancy: only in Philadelphia and Charleston were pieces occasionally made that closely reproduced Chippendale's own designs. More typically, American furniture makers relied on simpler, outdated English forms—such as the sturdy cabriole leg and claw-and-ball foot—which they combined with modified versions of Chippendale's carving on chair backs, table stretchers, and high chest tops. Although Chippendale himself would not have considered such modifications "in the modern taste," they were fashionable by colonial standards, and continued to influence the design of both high-style and country furniture well after the designer's death in 1779.

Chippendale's designs, from *The Gentleman and Cabinet-Maker's Director.*

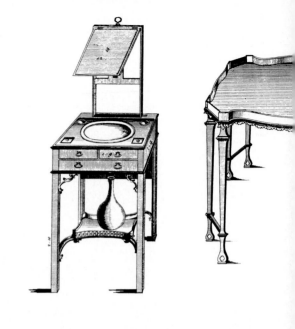

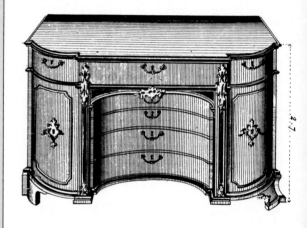

FEDERAL
1795-1815

Although American furniture makers still took their cues from England after the Revolution, the designs—in what is now known as the Federal style—were affected by a new consciousness that marked the beginning of American independence.

During the late 18th century, excavations at Pompeii and Herculaneum sparked a widespread fascination for classical antiquity, which symbolized the ultimate in civic virtue to the citizens of this newly formed nation. Soon, furniture took on the balanced proportions and symmetrical lines associated with classical design. Chairs boasted backs in the shape of shields and legs designed as fluted columns. Decorative elements, including urns, swags, and eagles, were also borrowed from classical design.

A Federal-period parlor like the one at left would typically have been decorated with classically inspired wallpaper and moldings, swag curtains, and a carpet that resembled a Roman tiled floor. Books on household management encouraged the use of decorative cotton dimity or chintz slipcovers to protect wool upholstery from insects and sun during the summer.

The Federal-style parlor at left, at Old Sturbridge Village in Massachusetts, is dressed for summer. The mahogany shield-back chairs were made in Boston; the center table and the piano date from around 1830, when the decor was updated.

EMPIRE: 1815-1840

During the Empire period, American furniture was influenced more by French style than by English design. While Napoleon ruled as Emperor of France (1804-1814), the delicate, classical furniture of the early 1800s was reinterpreted in heavier forms, with decorative carving and gilding and dark, richly grained wood veneers.

To mark the passage of France from republic to empire, and to commemorate Napoleon's campaigns in Egypt, French designers borrowed motifs from a wide range of classical and Egyptian subjects. Sphinx designs appeared as feet on table legs; the lyre became a familiar design for chair backs and table bases; and the Greek-inspired *klismos* chair—with its saber-shaped legs curved in opposing directions—became a standard for chair design. The new fashion in furniture swept Europe and England, and came to America in 1815.

At first, Empire furniture in America was available only to the wealthy in such centers as New York, Philadelphia, and Baltimore. But by the 1830s, far simpler adaptations were being produced inexpensively in towns throughout the East and Midwest. Furniture could now be made at least partially by machine in small factories, which kept production costs down. A different quality of Empire furniture was offered in every price range; and for the first time, it was possible for average homeowners to buy suites of furniture, such as the matching chairs and sofa in the Ohio parlor at left.

Just as the country was expanding during this period, Americans were inclined to build larger houses in the popular Greek Revival style, complete with spacious sitting rooms, parlors, and dining rooms. With its classical lines and massive proportions, Empire furniture was well suited to the new architecture.

In decorating, emphasis was placed on symmetry: mirrors were mounted between windows, tables were flanked by chairs, small pictures were hung in pairs. The first American guidebooks for decorating also appeared, enabling homeowners across the country to keep abreast of what signified good taste.

This Empire-style parlor at Shandy Hall in Geneva, Ohio, has been left as it was furnished by the owner, Robert Harper, in 1830. The furniture, including chairs, a horsehair sofa, and a lyre-base table, was ordered from such manufacturing centers as Cleveland and Buffalo. The pieces were veneered in walnut rather than the more expensive mahogany, but they still conveyed a look of elegance suitable to the home of an attorney and businessman.

The Hand at Work

*furniture from
the rural craftsman*

Until the mid-19th century, when mass-production began to change the nature of furniture making, many of the pieces used in rural American homes were the work of local craftsmen. The style and quality of the furniture that the craftsmen produced depended on the tastes and needs of their clientele, as well as on their own levels of skill in cabinetmaking and upholstery.

In general, country furniture was simpler than its high-style counterpart. Yet country craftsmen kept up with advances in cabinetmaking techniques, and the furniture they made in the period between the early 1700s and the mid-1800s shows the same evolution from necessity to comfort as does urban furniture. And like high-style pieces, country furniture came to include specialized forms such as desks, tall chests, and tea tables. The furniture is also often remarkably sophisticated, revealing the taste for colorful decoration and the strong sense of imagination that are hallmarks of country craftsmanship.

This painted Pennsylvania schrank, or wardrobe, was handcrafted around 1800.

In the country Chippendale chair above left, made by the Dominy family of Long Island, a stylish back crest was combined with old-fashioned turned stretchers. The circa 1780 chair above right, made by the Dunlap family of New Hampshire, features exaggerated ears.

In most 17th- and 18th-century rural settlements in America, tastes were conservative and changes came slowly. Even if a country dweller could have afforded a high-style chair from a furniture-making center like Boston or Philadelphia, such a piece may not have appealed to his taste, and would have looked decidedly out of place in his home.

As evidenced by the chairs above, made by four well-known craftsmen, much country furniture nevertheless displayed fine workmanship and design. In small communities, people were still style-conscious, and a well-established network of travel routes used by tradesmen brought them a knowledge of the fashions that were popular in more sophisticated regions.

While the country craftsman made simple, basic pieces, he also followed the furniture styles of the day. Using local woods, he simply adopted the most distinctive features of each new style—the vase-shaped back splat of the Queen Anne period, perhaps, or the claw-and-ball foot of the Chippendale style—and interpreted them in his own vernacular. In the process, he might change proportions and simplify details, or combine a new feature with an old form that was still used locally even though it had become outdated elsewhere.

The Country Craftsman

The country craftsman was not necessarily less skilled than his urban counterpart, but he may not have enjoyed the benefit of formal training. Moreover, unlike the urban cabinetmaker, who had far more customers—and buyers of higher means—and could afford to specialize, the rural craftsman had to make a living by practicing several trades at once. He might support his family simultaneously as a cabinetmaker, house-builder, mason, distiller, shoemaker, and of course, farmer.

The farm came first, however, and work was dictated by the seasons. The fields took precedence in the summer; furniture making was limited to winter and early spring. Even with tool in hand, the craftsman was as apt to build a wagon or a coffin as he was to make a chair.

Some skilled country woodworkers, however, did concentrate on establishing family businesses, training cousins, brothers, sons, and grandsons in their craft. The distinctive forms and characteristics that they developed for their furniture dominated the popular taste in their communities for generations. Such craftsmen served every strata of country society. Their pieces ranged from the simple to the sophisticated, and their names—well-known in their own time—are still remembered today.

The circa 1780 chair above left was made by the Connecticut craftsman Eliphalet Chapin. The Ohio Windsor chair above right is the work of William Tygert, whose imaginative design combined an arrow back with bamboo-turned legs.

Turned Chairs

Chairs with turned posts and stretchers exhibit different characteristics, depending on where and when they were made. The Connecticut heart-and-crown chair above left features prettily shaped turnings. The posts on the William and Mary chair above right are thick and solid. In the Queen Anne period, turnings on chairs like that at right could be quite slender.

Chairs made with turned posts and stretchers were among the earliest types in America. In woodworking, "turning"—the technique used to shape the wood—refers to work done on a lathe. The operation of this relatively complex tool called for the efforts of two men: a hired hand or an apprentice cranked a large wheel that powered the lathe; the craftsman held a chisel to the wood as it turned.

Shaping spindles, stretchers, and posts of uniform size and design required extensive practice. Once a craftsman became skillful, however, turning was the quickest, most efficient way to make chairs. Separate parts could be turned out one after another and assembled later: holes were simply cut into the posts with an auger, and the stretchers were inserted and glued. And, if a particularly pleasing shape emerged on the lathe, the craftsman could make a template from it and repeat the design.

Joined Chairs

By the 1730s, furniture began to take on lighter proportions. Although the tradition for making turned chairs continued in rural areas for several decades, newly fashionable joined chairs with flat, shaped posts were also made. The process of crafting flat furniture parts was slower, more laborious, and far more expensive than turning. Each piece was cut with a saw, then refined with a drawknife—a two-handled tool used for shaving a surface—and a plane. Also, the tops of the posts had to be matched carefully to the top crest, which was attached by means of mortise-and-tenon joints.

New methods of design and joinery usually appeared first in the most prominent parts of a chair—the back and crest. To save on the cost of producing a chair, a craftsman might combine a stylish new back with traditional turned legs and stretchers long after turnings were considered old-fashioned.

The maker of the country Queen Anne chair above left combined a fashionable joined back with an earlier style of turned legs. The cabriole legs on the joined Chippendale chair above right had to be individually shaped and carved, which added considerably to the cost of the piece. The design of the country Chippendale chair at left features simple carved legs with a joined back.

THE WINDSOR

If any one furniture form could be singled out as the most characteristically American, it would probably be the Windsor chair. By the time of the Revolution, the Windsor had become the most popular furnishing in the colonies. It appealed to all strata of society—it was used in gardens, on porches, in farmhouses, town houses, and public buildings alike—and remains a favorite today. The Windsor chairs at right are some of the many variations—named for their different back designs—made in America between about 1765 and 1820.

The term Windsor refers to a type of furniture, also called stick furniture, that is made primarily of posts and spindles. In a Windsor chair, lathe-turned legs and back spindles are socketed into a solid plank seat, and a steam-bent hoop is often used for the arm or back rails—a construction method that owes its beginnings more to the craft of wheel making than to that of furniture making. Because several different woods were often used in the same chair, most Windsors were painted, although many have since been stripped.

The Windsor chair is believed to be named for the town of Windsor, England, one of several places where such furniture was first made, around the turn of the 17th century. The earliest examples produced in the colonies, comb-backs, were made in Philadelphia around 1730. That city became the center of Windsor production, and by mid-century Philadelphia chairs were being

Perhaps the earliest American Windsor, Philadelphia, c. 1730

Rare, braced comb-back side chair, Philadelphia, 1740-1760

Comb-back highchair, Philadelphia, c. 1750

Fan-back side chair, Philadelphia, 1765-1780

Child's fan-back side chair, Connecticut, c. 1790

Writing-arm comb-back chair, Connecticut, c. 1790

Continuous-arm chair, New York, 1780-1800

Upholstered bow-back side chair, Philadelphia, c. 1790

Bow-back armchair, probably Maryland, 1790-1810

Low-back armchair, Philadelphia, c. 1760, with early paint

Comb-back armchair, Philadelphia, 1765-1780

Braced fan-back armchair, Philadelphia, 1765-1780

Child's sack-back armchair, Philadelphia, 1760-1770

Sack-back armchair, Lancaster County, Pennsylvania, c. 1765

Sack-back armchair, Philadelphia, 1765-1780

Bow-back side chair, Rhode Island, c. 1790

Child's rod-back armchair, New Hampshire, 1800-1820

Rod-back side chair, New England, 1800-1820

shipped all along the eastern seaboard and to the West Indies. Other important centers for Windsor chair making were located in New York, Rhode Island, and Connecticut.

Philadelphia craftsmen introduced new designs from England, such as the sack-back in the 1760s and the bow-back in the 1780s. At the same time, they altered the English designs, adapting local turning patterns used on slat-back chairs. Another refinement was the tapered leg, which, as production increased, was more expedient to craft than the cylinder-and-ball-foot leg used on the earliest Windsors. As designs were modified, the chairs could be made affordable to most people.

In the 1780s, a New York chairmaker perfected a steam-bending process in which the back and arms of the bow-back form were shaped from a single piece of wood, instead of attached separately as in the Philadelphia bow-back chairs. This unique American design became immensely popular and was produced widely—although never by chairmakers in Philadelphia.

The last major design change in the Windsor came in the early 19th century with the rod-back chair. Introduced from England, its simple, rectangular form featured bamboo-like rods for the back posts and crest rails as well as for the legs. The 19th century signaled a new unity for Windsor design. As mass production of these chairs increased in the mid-1800s, designs became simplified and less varied.

In the 1830s and 1840s,
many manufacturers
produced inexpensive
painted and stenciled chairs
like the original, signed
Hitchcock chair above left.
The green settee, center, is
decorated with stenciled
flower and fruit designs
typical of those favored
in the 1840s.

From the time that furniture was first made in the colonies, paint was a commonly used finish. Nearly all 17th-century furniture, in fact, was painted, and as early as the 1680s, professional painters, who ground their own pigments and made their own brushes, were setting up shops in prosperous towns along the east coast.

Paint not only protected the wood, but also provided color in houses where there was little other ornament. Much of the furniture made in the 1600s was finished in solid colors—mainly brown, black, and reddish brown. Some pieces, such as blanket chests and elaborate cupboards, however, were decorated with colorful painted

detail meant to show off fine carving, or with ornate patterns designed to imitate the dimensional look of carving. Indeed, imitative painting was considered highly fashionable; appreciated as an art in itself, it was used to decorate furnishings and woodwork alike.

By far the most popular form of decorative painting was grain-painting, which on 18th-century furniture ranged from close imitations of genuine wood grain to highly imaginative designs that were intended to be ornamental rather than realistic. Both types of grain-painting—which might or might not be done by a professional—involved a process in which the painter swirled, dabbed, or otherwise marked a pattern

Decorative Painting

into wet paint with a feather, comb, sponge, wadded paper or cloth, or perhaps his fingers.

During the Chippendale period, decorative painted finishes lost popularity somewhat, in favor of carving. However, furniture continued to be painted in bright and dark solid colors in rural areas, and a general interest in decorative painting was revived during the Federal period. The delicate, classically inspired furniture favored at this time was often painted in soft colors and enhanced with thin striping or hand-painted "fancywork" scenes and flowers. Federal furniture also featured pretty woods and inlays, which were imitated in paint in areas where fine imported woods were hard to get.

By around 1810, interest in graining was such that even the high-style furniture of urban areas was painted to imitate decorative woods such as rosewood, and was further embellished with gold-leaf or gilt-paint decoration. Gilding was costly, but by the early 19th century, inexpensive bronze powders that could be applied with stencils had become available. Stenciling with colored or metallic powders required far less skill than hand-painting, and the process caught on quickly. By the 1820s, factories such as the Hitchcock Factory of Barkhamsted (now Riverton), Connecticut, were capitalizing on the trend, mass-producing painted and bronze-stenciled chairs for as little as $1.25 apiece.

The "roundabout," or corner, chair above is decorated with the red-and-black grain-painting that was popular during the early 18th century. Although paint was sometimes used to disguise inexpensive woods, on this country chair, it was added purely as stylish decoration—as were the carved feet.

The blades on the circa 1830 Ohio rocker above left were probably added after the chair itself was made. The painted, circa 1830 Windsor above right was made with a high back and an extra-tall comb crest for resting the head.

The rocking chair is among the most familiar forms of seating furniture in this country, but it is unclear how or when it first evolved. One fact is certain, however: rocking chairs are a purely American innovation.

The ledgers of early furniture makers suggest that Americans may have started using rockers as early as the 1740s. The first known examples, dating from about the 1750s, are ladder-back chairs to which rocker blades were added. Converting chairs into rockers (a practice that continued into the 19th century) required trimming a few inches off the rear legs so that the chair would tilt back slightly; a notch was usually cut into the outside edge of each leg to keep the rocker blade in place.

By the late 1700s, it had become common for tall-back Windsor armchairs to be designed expressly as rockers. The legs were left thick rather than tapered; a slot was cut into the bottom of each leg, and a thin rocker blade, or "carpet cutter," was inserted. In the 1800s, the legs were more commonly tapered to points that could be set into thick rocker blades.

Many Windsor rockers were decorated with paint, an idea that was picked up by Lambert Hitchcock, who first mass-produced rockers in his Connecticut factory around 1800. Hitchcock

Rocking Chairs

rockers, based on Windsor styles, were available in solid black, yellow, white, and grain-painted finishes embellished with painted scenes or bronze stenciling. This decoration helped promote a fashion for "fancywork" chairs.

One of the most popular "fancy" styles was the Boston rocker, which—despite its name—was produced by Hitchcock and other non-Boston manufacturers beginning in 1825, and may in fact have originated in Connecticut. The rolled seat and curled arms that are the hallmarks of the Boston rocker were designed for comfort, while its broad crest and seat front offered ample space for the scenic paintings and stenciled cornucopias and baskets of fruit that were the favored decorations.

A plainer style of rocker shared popularity with the Boston rocker in the 19th century. By 1830, the Shaker community in New Lebanon, New York, had perfected a simple, slat-back rocking chair that was a model of comfort and balanced design. From the mid-1800s until the 1930s, the Shakers produced these chairs for sale to "the world," making them in seven sizes. Shaker rockers won awards at the 1876 Philadelphia Centennial for "strength, sprightliness, and modest beauty," qualities for which they are still admired today.

The high back and curved seat of the 1825 Boston rocker above left was designed for relaxed rocking. The 1858 swivel-seat Shaker rocker above right is believed to be the only one of its kind ever made.

Country
Easy Chairs

A late-1700s New England craftsman used planks of pine in his country version of the easy chair, above left. The easy chair above right retains its original foundation of ticking and linen, and would have had a slipcover.

The first truly comfortable seating form in the colonies was the wing chair, or "easy chair," as it was traditionally called. Introduced from England around 1700, easy chairs were not found in parlors during the 18th century, but instead were placed in bedrooms. The tall, winged back fended off drafts, and the down-filled cushion seat and upholstered frame allowed sitters to doze in comfort by the fire.

Easy chairs were extremely expensive: up-holstering was a technique practiced by highly trained specialists, fabric was costly, and building the frames required skillful craftsmanship. Few people in rural areas could afford the luxury of owning a chair made in this way. The easy chair was nevertheless in demand, and country craftsmen copied the form in wood or produced simple frame-and-upholstery versions. Although relatively unsophisticated, country easy chairs still helped keep drafts off the sitter's back.

Colonial Upholstery

Upholstered furniture was a luxury in colonial times, and the trade of the upholsterer was a prestigious, profitable, and varied one. Like a modern-day interior designer, an upholsterer coordinated much of the fabric decoration in a house, including bed hangings, table coverings, and draperies. His primary responsibility, however, was to fit out the frame of an easy chair or a sofa—traditionally constructed by a cabinetmaker—with a resilient foundation that not only made the piece comfortable but was essential in defining its overall form. He also made the final choices for the fabric finishings, which included permanent fitted coverings as well as loose "cases," or slipcovers.

The job of fitting the frame began with the supports; in fact, the name "upholsterer" derives from the term "upholder," which in 17th-century England referred to the craftsman who produced the webbing and cushioning materials for a furniture piece that "upheld" the sitter. First, a network of webbing was nailed to the wooden frame (springs were not used until the 1820s). Next, a linen lining was tacked over this webbed sling; then came a stuffing of hair, straw chaff, wool, or feathers. This stuffing was sandwiched in place by another layer of linen and was secured by rows of stitching. The piece was then ready to receive its finishing fabric.

Among the early upholstery materials used in the colonies was leather: both "Russian" leather, which was made by a special curing process, and calf leather provided durable coverings. A hard-wearing alternative was Turkey work, a knotted pile fabric similar to Middle Eastern carpets. Another choice was canvas decorated with needlework such as crewel or needlepoint.

Some furniture, however, was upholstered with such fabrics as wool and silk damask, velvet, wool plush, and worsteds. Haircloth, a woven blend of horsehair and cotton, was also widely used, because it was both strong and moth-resistant.

To hold the covering in place, upholsterers added rows of brass nails, called garnishing, as well as ribbon, tape, or welting. Pieces might also be trimmed with such decorative touches as tassels, braids, ruffles, or fringe.

Practical Tables

Rooms in colonial houses served multiple purposes, and furnishings—frequently moved from room to room—were equally adaptable. Small tables, for example, were generally sturdy, but still light enough to be carried. Some were cleverly designed as convertible pieces that could serve as either table or chair.

Small 18th-century tables made with stretchers bracing the four legs, as in the examples above, are known as tavern tables today. But while they certainly were used in taverns, they were more often found in houses. Fitted with oval or rectangular tops—and made with or without drawers—these low tables were as convenient for writing as they were for serving tea.

Often painted black or reddish brown, tavern tables frequently had maple bases and pine tops. The most highly prized examples are distinguished by bold turnings, splayed legs, and a decoratively cut-out skirt. "Brush," or Spanish,

feet were the marks of particularly stylish tables in the early 18th century. But because such carved feet were more difficult and expensive to make than simple turned feet, they are comparatively rare.

Chair-tables, based on English designs, were listed in American household inventories as early as 1650. The first types had heavily turned legs and were made of oak, with a pine top and seat. Usually painted, they were considered fashionable enough for use in parlors. Made with round, oval, rectangular, or octagonal tops that pivoted on wooden pegs, these tables were generally moved from the side to the center of a room and used at mealtime. With the top flipped back, as in the chair-table opposite, they were placed against the wall and used as seating. Chair-tables with lighter turnings or simple, square legs continued to be made until the end of the 18th century, and the form was revived again in the mid-1800s.

Made of tiger maple and hard pine, the chair-table above remained in the same family for many years.

The unique folk-art painting depicts the family homestead in 1777, when the table was made.

Drop-Leaf Tables

The walnut gate-leg table, top, was made in the Chesapeake area of Virginia around 1720. The small, maple butterfly table, bottom, was originally painted black and was made in Massachusetts between 1710 and 1740.

Drop-leaf tables—made with hinged tops that fold down—have been used in America since the late 1600s. One of the earliest types, the gate-leg table, was common from around 1690 to 1725. Gate-leg tables were generally made of walnut or maple and were solidly built with four turned stationary legs connected by stretchers. Two additional legs swing out—like gates—to support the leaves.

Around 1710, the butterfly table, an American innovation, was devised. Usually smaller than gate-leg tables, butterfly tables were named

for the wing-shaped leaf supports that pivot out from the stretchers.

Between 1730 and 1790 swing-leg tables—hinged along the rails—were the most popular form of drop-leaf table. Although this type was more graceful-looking than the gate-leg table, it was less sturdy, as it had only two fixed legs.

The Pembroke table, fashionable from the late 18th century until about 1815, was made with leaf supports that were hinged to the rail, but its four legs were stationary. These tables were used for breakfast or games.

The 1730s Virginia swing-leg table, top, has only one drop leaf and was made to fit into a corner. The cherry Pembroke table, bottom, was made in Massachusetts in 1805.

47

The country Queen Anne tea table above left was made in Connecticut between 1730 and 1770. Although it is simple in form, the particularly bright paint makes it remarkable. The circa 1835 server above right was dramatically painted to imitate inlaid Federal furniture of the period.

As the colonists became settled and prosperous, their houses gradually grew in size and their furnishings increased in number. The practice of carrying small tables from one room to another came to an end as people began to use rooms and furniture for specific purposes. Stylish little tables like those above, designed for both work and leisure activities, were not necessities; consequently, owning one reflected a homeowner's ability to afford the latest designs.

During the 1700s, one of the most fashionable of such tables was the tea table. Early in the century, imported Chinese tea was a rare and expensive luxury, but by the 1740s its price had dropped, and tea drinking—considered highly exotic—had become quite popular. The Queen Anne tea table—such as the painted piece above left, inspired by Chinese tables with cabriole legs—quickly became the preferred piece of furniture for setting out a tea service. Because tea drinking required costly pots, sugar bowls, and porcelain cups, tea tables were often designed with raised rims to protect such finery from breakage.

By 1800, during the Federal period, dining rooms started to become common in houses. Along with the appearance of large dining tables came sideboards and small servers that were placed against the wall. Typically such pieces had splashboards—to protect the wall from splashes when liquids were poured—and drawers for storing utensils and linens. The decorative server above, second from left, is painted to imitate the fancy inlays that were used on high-style pieces, while the trompe l'oeil oval panels on its drawer were most likely intended to suggest the side doors that frequently ap-

Specialized Tables

peared on larger, more sophisticated sideboards.

Specialized tables were also designed expressly for card playing and other games. While such tables were produced as early as 1720 in the colonies, they did not become common parlor furnishings until the Federal period. It was at this time that card parties in private houses became popular social occasions. Either square or circular, card tables typically had a folding top, hinged at the back, and a rear leg that could swing out to support the top when it was open. When the tables were not in use, the tops were folded back and the tables placed out of the way against a wall. Country card tables were often quite fashionable: carved mahogany was a favorite material in the 18th century, and delicate inlays were a popular decoration in the 1800s. Made of cherry, the card table directly above was originally stained a darker color to resemble the more expensive, more desirable mahogany.

A variety of small workstands also became prevalent during the Federal period. Designed with one or two drawers, and occasionally with drop leaves, workstands were a convenient size for holding sewing tools. On fancier stands, such as the handsome mahogany piece directly above, a roomy bag made of gathered or pleated fabric was attached under the lower drawer, which usually had no bottom: when the drawer was pulled open, one's sewing could be easily dropped from sight. Many such workstands were distinguished by the delicate turned or tapered legs that characterized Federal-style furnishings. These pieces were made of distinctively grained woods such as tiger maple, used for the stand above right, or were ornamented with lively painted decoration.

The cherry card table above left was made in Massachusetts around 1792. The 1810 sewing stand above center is made of mahogany and mahogany veneer; the fabric bag is green silk. The 1820s workstand above right is bird's-eye maple.

The simple maple William and Mary stand above left is distinguished by a "dished" top, as is the tiger maple Federal stand above center. The circa 1760 "birdcage" stand above right has a top that can pivot as well as tilt; such pieces took longer to make than standard tilt-top stands and were consequently more expensive.

Commonly known as candlestands today, small tables supported by a pedestal, or pillar—and usually a tripod base—originally were used for many purposes, including serving tea, writing letters, and playing games.

Such stands were made continually from the 17th century until the mid-19th century and display the characteristics of the various popular furniture styles. The turned legs of the William and Mary period, for example, evolved into the cabriole legs of the Queen Anne and Chippendale periods, and eventually became the simple tapered legs of the Federal period.

Although stands were meant to be practical and were certainly not the most important pieces of furniture in a house, care was often lavished on their design. They were usually highly sculptural and elegant in appearance. The turned shapes of the pedestals, the height of the legs,

and the size and placement of drawers—when drawers were included—all contribute to the overall look of a stand.

The shape and decoration of the tops also add interest to these small stands. Circular and square tops are the most common, but oval, octagonal, and rectangular forms were also made. Most tops are simply flat and geometric in shape, but stylish pieces are apt to have added features: the "dished" rim that appears around the edge of circular stands; rounded and decoratively cut-out "porringer" corners; fine veneers; and even painted game boards.

Tilt-top stands, which had flip tops and could easily be placed out of the way in a corner, were a very popular type. Usually the top could simply flip up and down, but on fancy examples, the pedestal passed through a "birdcage," or columned block, that allowed the top to pivot as well as tilt.

Country Stands

Clockwise from top left are four stands made around 1800: a cherry stand with "porringer" corners; a stained maple stand painted with a yellow-and-black checkerboard; a cherry stand with maple inlay from the Connecticut Valley area; and a Massachusetts cherry stand with an ash, maple, and mahogany inlaid top.

With its paneling and shallow, overall carving, the oak chest, top, probably from Guilford, Connecticut, is typical of the paneled chests made in the mid-17th century. The circa 1760 Virginia chest, middle, displays an early style of construction marked by heavy corner stiles. The vibrant grain-painted chest, bottom, was made in Pennsylvania around 1830.

Early Chests

The blanket chest above was made in the area of Hadley, Massachusetts, between 1695 and 1720. Its colorful painted decoration imitates the carved designs that were also favored during that time.

Until closets became common around the mid-19th century, chests were especially important articles of furniture in American houses. Indeed, for 17th-century colonists, chests were indispensable, serving as extra seating, storage for blankets and clothing, and a place to lock away valuables.

Most 17th-century chests made in America resembled those of medieval England. Typically, they were built with paneled sides joined to solid corner stiles that extended down to form feet. The large flat surfaces of the panels and drawer fronts lent themselves to vivid carved and painted decoration, which often made such chests the most ornate pieces of furniture in 17th-century colonial homes. Carving in low relief was usually done by specialists. This flat style of carving remained popular in America until around 1720, long after it had ceased to be fashionable in England.

By the late 18th century, chests were usually made with flat sides, although painted decoration was sometimes used to imitate the earlier paneled construction. While many chests were painted simply with a single color, the tradition for using chests as showcases for decorative painting continued with the lively grain-painted designs of the 1800s.

GRAIN-PAINTING A CUPBOARD

The technique of grain-painting was commonly used for finishing furniture during the 18th and 19th centuries. In this process, a tinted glaze is applied over a solid base coat of paint, and then marked while still wet—usually with a comb, feather, wadded cloth, or the fingers—to create a pattern. The technique is easy to learn and can provide a distinctive decoration for a new unfinished piece.

The glaze used for the cupboard above consists of vinegar, paint pigments, and corn syrup; it is simple to prepare and takes about twenty minutes to dry. (For the best results, avoid glazing on a humid day.) Be sure to choose a vivid color—or colors—for the base coat, and tint the glaze a darker color than that used for the base. This cupboard was painted with black glaze over yellow and red base colors, and the pattern was created using the fingers and crumpled plastic wrap. To make other unusual patterns, try dabbing the paint with different areas of your hand, or with whatever is available—perhaps a piece of clay or sponge.

A. Glaze is brushed on evenly over all base colors; base colors should be bright enough to show through glaze.

B. Finger-pattern effect is achieved by pressing fingers into glaze; base color will show through where you press.

C. Crumpled plastic wrap is held at one corner of panel, then dabbed on in arc to achieve fan effect.

MATERIALS

· Unfinished wooden cupboard ·
· Latex primer (1 quart will cover a 34 x 44 x 18-inch cupboard) ·
· 1 quart semigloss latex paint for each base-coat color ·
· Light corn syrup ·
· Distilled white vinegar ·
· Dry pigments or poster paints for tinting glaze ·
· Large container for mixing glaze ·
· Two 3-inch paintbrushes · Two 2-inch paintbrushes ·
· Plastic wrap for graining ·
· 2 quarts satin-finish clear polyurethane varnish ·

DIRECTIONS

1. Using a 3-inch paintbrush, apply primer to cupboard. Let dry.

2. Using other 3-inch paintbrush, apply one coat of latex paint to cupboard for base coat. (Paint entire cupboard one color or paint selected areas in different colors.) Let dry. Apply second coat. Let dry thoroughly.

3. To prepare glaze, mix 1 teaspoon corn syrup, ¼ cup vinegar, and 2 teaspoons dry pigment or poster paint in container; blend well. Add more vinegar, a little at a time, until glaze is consistency of heavy cream. This will make about 1 cup, more than enough to glaze cupboard of size indicated above.

4. Using a 2-inch brush, apply glaze to cupboard front, limiting application to an area (such as door borders) that you can decorate in about 20 minutes. Brush on glaze until it is very smooth and semitransparent (Illustration A).

5. To achieve finger-pattern effect, while glaze is still wet, press into it lightly with fingers (Illustration B), then move fingers along. (Be careful not to press too hard or you will remove too much glaze. If glaze should become too dry, or if you don't like the pattern you have created, go over that section with brush slightly dampened with vinegar, and surface will be ready to rework.)

6. To achieve fan effect, use piece of plastic wrap about 6 inches long. Bunch plastic wrap, take ends in each hand, and pull taut. While glaze is still wet, hold one end of plastic wrap firmly against cupboard and dab other end around in arc (Illustration C). For sunburst effect, hold one end of plastic wrap firmly against cupboard and dab other end around in full circle.

7. Continue glazing and making patterns in small areas until surface of cupboard is decorated.

8. Let surface dry thoroughly, about 1 hour; the dried glaze should look dull. If you are not happy with the way grain-painting looks at this stage, simply remove glaze with paper towel dampened with vinegar, and start again.

9. To protect decoration, apply one coat varnish using other 2-inch brush. Let dry thoroughly. Apply second coat and let dry.

Chests of
Drawers

The 1700s chest above left was meant to be plain: the brasses, added some time after it was made, have

since been removed. The circa 1786 chest, top right, has a scalloped top unique to pieces made in the

Connecticut Valley. The William and Mary chest, bottom right, has typical teardrop pulls.

The end of the 17th century signaled a radical change in the way furniture was made in the colonies: cabinetry—in which dovetail joints were used to join relatively thin, light boards—replaced the earlier mortise-and-tenon joinery.

By the late 1600s, case furniture, which refers to caselike pieces made with drawers, had already begun to lose its low, horizontal look. The new cabinetry allowed case furniture to continue to extend upward, since such pieces could now be made lighter in weight.

By the 1730s, chests of drawers were commonly made. One of the most familiar styles was the four-drawer chest, in which the drawers were graduated in size, with the largest at the bottom. Such proportioning enhanced the vertical look, and helped keep a chest from appearing top-heavy. In some pieces, only the two lower drawers could be pulled out; the illusion of top drawers was created with paint and moldings,

and the chest actually had a lid that opened upward on hinges. As ceilings increased in height during the 1700s, chests became even taller; some were topped with a stepped pyramid made up of small drawers that was used for the display of pewter, porcelain, and silver.

On 17th-century chests, the thick corner stiles that held the chest together were simply extended downward as feet. With the introduction of cabinetry, the stiles were eliminated and the feet were attached separately. During the William and Mary period, heavy turned "bun" or "turnip" feet were favored. Flat cut-out "bracket" feet, mitered at the corners, had developed by the 1720s and continued to be used for the next hundred years. On fine Chippendale-style chests, made from about 1755 to 1795, short, carved cabriole legs appeared. And during the Federal period, both flat, tapered "French" feet and narrow turned legs became common on chests.

The French feet and painted "inlay" on the early-19th-century chest above left imitate the look of "fancy" Federal furniture. The 1820s chest above right is made of mahogany and pine and features reverse-painted glass panels and a lively cut-out splashboard.

High Chests of Drawers

The new emphasis on vertical forms in furniture in the early 18th century gave rise to the high chest, sometimes referred to as a highboy. Placed in the parlor or in bedrooms, early high chests were used to store clothes and linens, and to display valuable glass and porcelain on their flat tops. As houses became larger, and specialized furniture could be accommodated, high chests were usually made *en suite* with a matching dressing table.

Early high chests were designed with four drawers, and were set on a frame fitted with a single long drawer. As curved lines were introduced into furniture designs around 1700, the frames were given six turned legs, a "box" of stretchers, and turned "bun" feet. Because the legs were insecurely attached and broke easily, this form was short-lived. (The legs on most William and Mary chests have been replaced.)

With the arrival of the Queen Anne style, the bottom sections of high chests became taller, and cabriole legs were mortised to the sides of the chest, which ensured greater stability. Often built of walnut, cherry, or maple, early Queen Anne chests were typically made with flat tops and flaring cornice moldings. Although flat tops continued to appear until the late 1700s, more-stylish country high chests were designed with bonnet tops and turned finials from the 1750s onward; these embellishments added more curves and enhanced the vertical proportioning.

Stretcher bases like those on both of the William and Mary chests at right were a short-lived form.

The 1750s high chest above left is finished in walnut with sumac inlay; such veneering is rare on country

furniture. The rosettes on the circa 1775 chest above right are typical of Connecticut pieces.

Fall-Front Desks

The first desks in America were actually portable wooden boxes with hinged, slanted lids, and space within for books and papers. It was not until the early decades of the 18th century that desks evolved into actual pieces of furniture in themselves. A typical desk of this period was essentially a chest of drawers with a slanted lid—called a fall front—that pulled down to form a writing surface and to reveal a bank of small drawers and pigeonholes.

Fall-front desks were expensive articles of furniture, requiring a great deal of wood and the services of a skillful cabinetmaker. The desks were usually displayed in parlors, where they were placed near a window to take advantage of the natural light. Since the drawers and top compartment could be locked, desks were often used to store valuable belongings.

Around the 1730s, bookcase tops were added to desks for the safekeeping of business ledgers. Made with two paneled doors that locked, this tall form, now known as a secretary, was originally called a "desk and bookcase."

As on other types of furniture, the decorative elements of a desk displayed some variations in design, such as glass doors, and followed whatever furniture style was popular when the piece was made—the drop front was flat rather than slanted during the Federal period, for example. The basic form of the "desk and bookcase," however, remained very much the same.

Made in New England around 1840, the pine desk
at right has an unusually tall base and small top.

The decorative painting on the desk, top, resembles the crotched veneers of fine Federal furniture; the oval brasses are also typical of the period. Made of curly maple and tulip poplar, the country Empire desk, bottom, was made in Cincinnati around 1845.

The tiger maple "desk and bookcase" at right was made for a law office in Ohio in the late 1830s. The lower section of the desk was designed with two paneled doors rather than a series of drawers.

Made in New Hampshire in the latter half of the 18th century, the cherry Chippendale "desk and bookcase" at left displays an unusual interior, in which stacks of drawers take the place of the standard pigeonholes.

Above, left to right: an 1820 painted tall clock—a Pennsylvania piece with German works; a grained, circa 1840 clock with iron works; and a 1797 cherry clock made by Nathaniel Dominy on Long Island.

American Clocks

During the early colonial period, clocks were exceedingly rare in American households: few American clocks can be dated prior to the 1720s, and most were made after the Revolutionary War.

Most clocks were imported from England, but even if they were American made, they were expensive: each part of the works (known as the movement), as well as the case and dial, had to be crafted by hand. With the exception of a well-dressed bed, a clock was the most costly furnishing an individual was likely to buy. Watches were also scarce in the colonies and did not become an industry here until the 1840s. Anyone fortunate enough to own one would have hung it in a "watch hutch" at night; placed on a mantel or a bedside table, the watch hutch doubled as a clock.

The standard 18th-century timepiece was the tall clock. (These clocks were not called "grandfather clocks" until 1876, when a popular song, "My Grandfather's Clock," was published.) The tall case, consisting of a bonnet, shaft, and pedestal, was necessary for housing the pendulum,

which marked the seconds, and the weights, which propelled the works.

Clockmaking generally involved at least two craftsmen: a cabinetmaker, who created the case, and a clockmaker, who made and assembled the works and often signed the clock. The first American tall clocks had engraved brass dials imported from England. In the late 18th century, painted iron dials replaced the brass variety; they were easier to read and far less expensive to produce. Early painted dials were also imported, but gradually American clockmakers began working with painters here.

Clockmaking changed from craft to industry in 1807, when a Connecticut craftsman, Eli Terry, started manufacturing clocks with wooden works. By designing machinery that allowed him to mass-produce parts, Terry was able to turn out sixty clocks in a single day. As early as 1816, he was selling shelf and mantel clocks for fifteen dollars, about one sixth the cost of a tall clock. By 1840 American clock-makers were using brass works, and by 1845 the modern spring-wound mechanism replaced weights.

The production of shelf clocks started around 1816. The machine-carved steeple clock above left was made in Connecticut in 1845. The clock above center, by the well-known maker Silas Hoadley, has a reverse-painted glass door panel. The carved cherry watch hutch above right was made in Newport, Rhode Island, in 1765.

The Melting Pot

the rich ethnic heritage of America's settlers

I mmigrants to America during the 18th and 19th centuries generally arrived with no more than a few belongings. But each ethnic group also carried cultural "baggage"—religious beliefs, folkways, and design traditions—that had a direct impact on the furniture they crafted for their new homes.

Some groups, such as the Shakers, were united not by ancestry but by religious beliefs, and these ideas are clearly reflected in their furniture designs. Other groups, such as the conservative Germans in Pennsylvania, held fast to an established tradition of furniture making that remained relatively unchanged after it was transplanted to this country.

Most of America's early settlers, however, developed hybrid furniture styles: they introduced their own forms to this country—the German dower chest, the French armoire, the Norwegian log chair—and then adapted them to suit whatever materials might be available. The rich designs that resulted are as varied in character as the people who created them.

Shaker pieces like this washstand are devoid of "worldly" ornament.

Shaker Furniture

In 1774, Ann Lee, the founder of a group of religious separatists known as the United Society of Believers in Christ's Second Appearing, left England for America with eight followers. Their first community was formally established a few years later in Watervliet, New York, and the sect steadily gained members. By 1840, some six thousand Believers—also called Shakers because they shook, whirled, and danced while they worshiped—had settled in eighteen utopian communities from Maine to Kentucky.

The early furniture produced by the Shakers was essentially the same as that made by other cabinetmakers; in fact, when they first arrived here, the Shakers simply built whatever was necessary, drawing on local woodworking traditions. But as the movement gained momentum, the fundamentalist Christian values of the society began to shape a unique furniture style.

Indeed, with its designs based on simplicity and order, Shaker furniture—made primarily between 1790 and 1900—has been called "religion in wood" because it so completely reflects the beliefs of its makers. Woodworking, and all other labor, was considered a form of worship, and each piece of Shaker furniture was meant to express perfection in design by being functional rather than decorative. But while Shaker furniture is distilled to its simplest, most practical forms, it is not crude. Shaker craftsmen handled proportion, line, and color with skill.

Continued

Made around 1825 of pine and butternut,

the cupboard at right is a typical Shaker built-in.

Clockwise from top left: an 1843 sewing table fitted with a measuring stick; a circa 1825 stained cherry stand with typical spider legs; a circa 1825 stand with a drawer that can be opened from either side; and a circa 1821 painted chest with an extra drawer at its base.

The circa 1870 highchair, above, was designed for the children raised in Shaker communities. The celibate Shakers took in orphans as well as children arriving with their parents.

Instantly recognizable for its restrained lines, Shaker furniture also bears some trademarks developed by the Believers. Among these are flame and acorn finials on chair backs, "mushroom" posts on chair arms, colorful woven chair-seat tapes, and top rails for ladder-back rockers (over which a cushion or shawl could be hung). Only excessive ornamentation, such as carving, veneer, inlay, or molding that was not considered intrinsic to the design and function of the piece, was forbidden—it was deemed too "worldly."

Canny business people, the Shakers began to sell chairs from their workshops in the 1790s. Most of the furniture they made, however, was for their own use, and its forms were directly influenced by the communal nature of the society. Because the members worked, lived, dined, and worshiped in groups, their furnishings were often oversize: dining tables might be as long as twenty feet, benches and settees provided for multiple seating, and cupboards stretched from floor to ceiling. Some pieces also incorporated innovative features: beds, for example, were fitted with casters so that they could

be moved easily, and side chairs were built with special ball-and-socket devices, which allowed the sitter to tilt back without damaging the carpet.

Although uniformity in furniture design was a Shaker ideal, certain pieces were individualized. A special rocking chair might be made to size for an elderly or infirm Believer. And tables, chairs, and desks for Shaker sisters were constructed more delicately and with shorter legs than those for brothers.

Perhaps the most striking characteristic of Shaker furniture, however, is its timelessness. In effect, the Shakers had withdrawn from the "world" into their own communities in the belief that they were preparing for the millennium. Because they felt this "heaven on earth" would last a thousand years, they built furniture that was also meant to last; its solid construction and fine craftsmanship were a tribute to God. Clearly the Shakers achieved their mission, for today the modest, graceful designs of Shaker furniture are just as respected as they were when the pieces were made.

The light, unusually short bench, above center, was designed for use in a Shaker meetinghouse. The typical Shaker rocking chair, above right, has a practical cushion rail and a woven cotton-tape seat.

A SHAKER SEWING ROOM

Shaker life centered around a highly organized society in which the members undertook daily activities in groups. Each community contained specialized workshops where the Shakers gathered to make furniture, produce crafts and necessities, and take care of housekeeping matters.

A sewing room like the one at left would have been used by deaconesses, who were elected by each communal "family" to supervise the household. Here they would mend worn clothes and sew new garments.

Carefully planned, this sewing room reflects the Shaker sense of order and utility. There are plenty of built-in drawers to store fabrics and notions neatly out of sight, and as is typical, the efficient worktables were designed to allow two deaconesses to work together. The stand between the two rockers, for instance, features a dual-slide drawer that pulls out from either end. In the sewing desk against the wall, some drawers are accessible from the front and others from the right side of the piece; a sliding shelf extends the desk-top surface. The close groupings of furniture also suggest the companionable nature of the Shakers, a sociable people who, as their journals record, truly did enjoy working together.

The deaconesses' sewing room, left, is located at Hancock Shaker Village in Pittsfield, Massachusetts.

One of the finest examples of Pennsylvania-German artistry, this walnut schrank

bears the name of its original owner. The sulfur-inlaid decorations are adapted from textile designs.

Pennsylvania-German Furniture

The black walnut side chair, far left, was made between 1730 and 1740 in Germantown, the first German settlement in Pennsylvania. It has turned members typical of German baroque pieces. The walnut and oak plank chair, near left, initialed and dated 1770, features a carved stag on its scrolled back. Plank chairs are also called Moravian chairs, since many surviving examples have come from communities founded by the Moravians, a sect that settled in Bethlehem, Pennsylvania.

From 1683 until the middle of the 18th century, some one hundred thousand German-speaking people left the war, taxation, and religious persecution of their homelands to settle outside Philadelphia in William Penn's tolerant Quaker colony. By the late 1700s, these immigrants constituted one third of Pennsylvania's population.

A diverse lot, they included both peasant farmers and skilled artisans, orthodox Lutherans and pietists such as the Amish. Yet, as a group, they were unified by language, customs rooted in medieval German culture, and a determination to preserve the folk traditions of their native lands.

Pennsylvania-German furniture is a product of these traditions, which were tempered by the limited resources and difficult living conditions in the New World. Made predominantly between the mid-1700s and the early 1800s, it is utilitarian, conservative, and expressive of the beliefs of these religious, industrious people.

Early Pennsylvania-German furniture was necessarily simple. As the settlers struggled to establish themselves, they furnished their log cabins with built-in beds, tables, and benches that were strictly functional in design and appearance. Once their farms began to prosper in the fertile piedmont between the Delaware and Susquehanna rivers, however, the Germans could afford to build spacious fieldstone homes and indulge their taste for the fine, gaily decorated furniture they had left behind in Europe.

Many skilled woodworkers had settled in the

Continued

The Pennsylvania-German slant-top desk, above left, of tulip poplar, is an example of Mahantango Valley craftsmanship. It is inscribed "Jacob Maser 1834"—the owner's name and marriage year. The 1803 dower chest, above right, is painted with intricate symbolic motifs, including unicorns, tulips, and birds.

colony by the mid-1700s, and they tended to re-create the solid baroque forms found in the furniture of their homeland. Still, they could not help but be influenced by their new surroundings. Not only did furniture makers learn to work such native woods as black walnut, cherry, maple, and tulip poplar, but freed from guild restrictions, they also began to express their individualism and love of color with hybrid forms and particularly vivid decoration.

While artisans crafted everything from small boxes to large sawbuck tables, they are perhaps best known for the three traditional furniture forms they introduced to Pennsylvania: the plank chair, the *schrank* (or wardrobe), and the dower chest. Based on a medieval prototype, the plank chair, or *brettstuhl,* is a sturdy stool with splayed stick legs, a flat seat, and a curved back often decorated with carving. Most Pennsylvania-German homes had few of them, however,

since built-in benches served as seating, and the busy farmers often preferred to eat standing up.

A *schrank,* on the other hand, could be found in almost every home. Since closets were uncommon—especially in stone houses—a *schrank* was designed to hold clothing for the entire family. *Schränke* generally had double doors over drawers, and were fitted inside with shelves and pegs. The finest examples were made of black walnut, a straight-grained, lustrous hardwood, and decorated with either carving or a unique sulfur inlay intended to suggest expensive wood marquetry.

Less elaborate *schränke* were made of pine and often painted—a favorite method of decoration in both southern Germany and Pennsylvania. Among the decorative motifs commonly used in this country were stylized tulips and other flowers, birds, hearts, and geometric shapes that could be easily scribed with a compass. Such

symbolic designs were derived from illuminated manuscripts, heraldic devices, and imagery in illustrated poems and hymns.

Perhaps the most recognizable and common Pennsylvania-German furniture form, however, is the dower chest, or *ausschteier kischt*. Such chests were made primarily between the 1770s and 1815. Whereas the *schrank* was a family piece, chests were designed for an individual and were often personalized with the owner's name and the date of presentation incorporated into the surface decoration. An owner might also mark a chest as his or her own by pasting a *fraktur*—a birth certificate, copybook exercise, or other folk calligraphy—to the inside of the lid.

Generally built of tulip poplar or pine, chests usually featured bracket feet, drawers along the base, and a roomy interior often fitted with a till (a small tray to hold valuables). While dower chests might be made for young men, they were

primarily given by fathers to their daughters, who used them to store linens and other trousseau items in preparation for married life. Chests made for girls were often lavishly painted with images relating to love and marriage, including hearts for love, pomegranates for fertility, doves for wedded bliss, lilies for virtue, and unicorns for chastity.

In the early 19th century, Pennsylvania-German furniture design began losing its strong Germanic lines, as westward-migrating pioneers of different ethnic backgrounds brought outside influences to the once insular communities. One isolated pocket of German craftsmen in the central Mahantango Valley along the Susquehanna River, however, did continue to work in the traditional forms until the 1830s. This furniture is noted for its modified Federal style, bright colors, and finely detailed paintings of trees, fans, horses, birds, and stars.

The circa 1820 chest of drawers, above left, combines both paneling and paintings of birds and angels as decoration. The hanging corner cupboard, above right, of yellow pine, was made in the late 1700s and was originally painted red. It was probably used to hold the family Bible, hymnal, and other religious books.

*Measuring 85 by 88 inches, this massive circa 1790 pine schrank from Lancaster County, Pennsylvania,
is decorated with painted floral motifs and marbleizing, and has fancy iron rat-tail hinges.*

This circa 1830 Pennsylvania-German cupboard has upper shelves with grooves and slots for displaying crockery and cutlery. Its scrolled and reeded decoration is emphasized with paint.

Norwegian-
American
Furniture

*The butternut chest of drawers, above left, from northern Minnesota, is dated 1872. The three-legged chair, or **bandestol**, above right, was designed to remain stable on uneven packed-dirt floors.*

Of all the Scandinavian immigrants, the Norwegians clung most tightly to the traditions of their homeland after coming to America. A proudly nationalistic people who had long suffered foreign rule, they began arriving in this country in 1825. By the early 1900s, a million Norwegians had relocated here, settling primarily in the upper Midwest.

Woodworking skills were central to the Norwegian way of life, and once here, the immigrants continued to make furniture similar to that which they had crafted in their own country. One such furniture form was the *kubbestol*, a type of chair that dates back to at least the 11th century. Made from a hollowed-out solid log, the *kubbestol* was fitted with a plank seat.

Another tradition perpetuated by the Norwegian immigrants was *rosemaling*, a type of decorative painting based on stylized flower and leaf motifs, which first became popular around 1750. *Rosemaling* was applied to such large furniture pieces as chests, beds, and cupboards. The designs were often inspired by images in picture books and illustrated Bibles, and they were interpreted differently in various Norwegian settlements.

The vintage bench, above left, was decorated with rosemaling in 1982 by a descendant of a Norwegian immigrant; the kubbestol, above right, was made in Minnesota in 1925; and the walnut cradle, left, was crafted in the mid-19th century.

Creole Furniture

The Louis XV-style cherry armoire, right, was made in Louisiana around 1800. It features the elaborate brass fiche hinges and scrolled escutcheons typical of French cabinetry, as well as an inlaid eagle motif adapted from Anglo-American pieces of the Federal period.

The French-speaking immigrants who settled along the Mississippi River in the 1700s and early 1800s hailed from France, Canada, and the Caribbean. While the Caribbean culture is thought to have influenced architectural design, it is the French provincial and French-Canadian heritage that is most evident in the furniture of this region. Very little of this so-called Creole furniture remains today; it was lost to the humid climate and replaced with more refined pieces in the 19th century.

The major contribution of the French settlers was the armoire, a variation on the wardrobe. Using indigenous cypress and hardwoods, such as cherry and walnut, and mahogany from the West Indies, local craftsmen created elegant armoires with cabriole legs, rounded cornices, and scalloped skirts. The inlaid motifs on many such pieces reflected an Anglo-American influence.

A number of distinctive chair styles are also associated with the Creoles, including a range of ladder-back chairs with ornately shaped or angular slats. Due to the damp climate, such chairs were often fitted with woven rush seats rather than upholstered seats. Another unique chair, the campeachy chair, which usually had a leather-sling seat, was one of the few Creole furniture forms to show Spanish influence.

The circa 1820 walnut and leather campeachy chair, above left, takes its name from the state of Campeche on the Yucatán Peninsula, where such chairs originated. The ladder-back armchair of cherry, above right, was made around 1815 in New Orleans.

The colorful trastero at right is typical of cupboards from the Southwest that were made and decorated specifically for the tourist market in the early 20th century. The pine piece displays motifs adapted from local textile patterns.

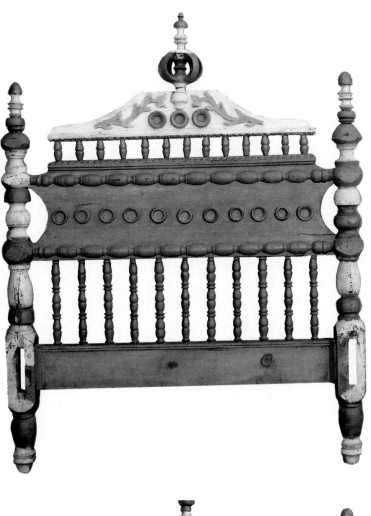

New Mexico Hispanic Furniture

New Mexico Hispanic furniture was influenced by three very different peoples: the native Indians, the 16th-century Spanish conquistadors, and the Anglo-American settlers of the mid-1800s. Scattered widely in the wilderness of New Mexico's northern Rio Grande Valley, the early settlers had few tools and limited materials for making furniture. Their unique pieces were born of necessity and remained relatively unaffected by the changes in furniture styles in Spain and its South American and Mexican empire for over two centuries.

Spain claimed the New World under its crown in 1493, and established its first permanent New Mexican colony—with soldiers, Franciscan missionaries, and seven Mexican and Spanish *carpinteros* (woodworkers)—in 1598. Trained in strictly regulated guilds, these *carpinteros* introduced the first metal hand tools to the continent. Using adzes, axes, knifelike saws, and chisels, the craftsmen interpreted traditional Spanish furniture forms in local ponderosa pine, a soft, easily worked wood. Both the missionaries and the *carpinteros* taught the Indians to use European tools and to build Spanish-style furniture.

The Spanish tradition of furnishing the home sparsely was continued in the 17th- and 18th-century houses and missions of New Mexico. Simple adobe dwellings were often appointed with no more than a few chests and stools, and

Continued

The head and foot boards, left, were made around 1870 by a master turner as a gift for his bride.

85

The armchair above, made in 1917, shows the open mortise-and-tenon joint construction common in Spanish colonial pieces, as well as the influence of California Mission style. The chair's carved decoration, highlighted with paint, derives from designs on 18th-century chests.

backless benches doubled as tables. Storage niches were built into walls and fitted with cupboard doors, and ledges protruded from the walls to serve as beds and additional benches.

Wealthier settlers could also afford one of the most distinctive pieces of furniture to be made in the Southwest—the *trastero*, or freestanding cupboard. The *trastero* is unique among such case pieces because its two upper doors were fitted with grills made of spindles or pierced wood panels, while sometimes the two lower doors were solid. *Trasteros* were used to hold utensils, as well as food, which was stored behind the ventilated upper doors.

New Mexico Hispanic furniture, especially the seating pieces, is characterized by a blocky style. This is the result of a proportion system that guild-trained woodworkers were required to follow. The system was based on the *vara*, a Spanish linear unit equaling roughly a yard. Most chairs were one *vara* high by one-half *vara* wide.

Also contributing to the sturdy look of this furniture is the joinery technique used almost exclusively among *carpinteros*. Chairs, benches, and tables were built of soft pine with open mortise-and-tenon joints, and this construction method became part of the overall design. Because the arid climate caused wood to shrink, pegs and shims were used to further strengthen the joints. (Iron nails were never used, since they might split the soft wood.)

New Mexico Hispanic furniture was deco-

rated with carvings that reflected a variety of techniques. Both shallow and deep relief carving were used to depict such motifs as rosettes, pomegranates, shells, and lions, favored by the Spanish. Shallow incising and chip carving were used to create circles and other geometric designs. The stepped carving often seen on the ends of chair and bench uprights symbolized heaven and rain in Indian mythology.

Furniture in the Southwest began to change rapidly in 1821, when the Santa Fe Trail opened. With the influx of Anglo-American traders, gold seekers, and soldiers following America's occupation of New Mexico in 1846, a market was created for furniture in the curvilinear Empire style popular in the eastern states.

At first, only Anglo-American cabinetmakers made pieces in this European-inspired style. But by the 1870s, Hispanic craftsmen began to incorporate Anglo-American features into their traditional furniture designs and to produce new forms, such as desks and center tables.

Turned spindles replaced carved chair splats, and beds were used instead of the customary mattresses laid out on the floor. The introduction of the lathe, molding plane, and frame also made possible more elaborate decoration, including cut-out panels, applied ornament, and grooved molding. The subdued mineral- and plant-base paint colors once used to emphasize carved motifs were replaced by bright polychrome decoration, grain-painting, and marbleizing.

Both the 19th-century bench, above center, and the side chair, above right, feature carving in the Indian-influenced stepped design. The bench, however, also displays Anglo-American influence with its scalloped skirt and vase-shaped splats. The carved motifs on the chair rails and posts were inspired by Spanish and Indian folklore.

SOUTHWEST STYLE

The contrasting hues of the painted desert; the brilliant blue of a vast, open sky; red clay earth; tall ponderosa pines. These are images from the American Southwest, a region that has inspired its own indigenous decorating style.

Even if you don't live in the Southwest, you can still get the regional look with the many southwest-style furnishings that are available today. Start with a few accessories—a woven throw, some clay pots, and a couple of cactus plants, perhaps—then gradually build a collection like that shown at right.

The key is to choose pieces rich in color—a brilliant red chair or a turquoise table, for example—then surround them with the soft, sunbleached shades of adobe and bone. There are no rules here; even twigs, skulls, and stones look right at home in this earthy setting.

Elements of southwest style: vintage furniture like the low table and blue hutch mix well with a room full of contemporary southwest-style pieces. From left, a rustic bench, a folding screen fashioned from multihued twigs, a red chair painted with American Indian motifs, the ubiquitous southwestern ladder—a necessity in multi-level Indian pueblos—a white-painted Taos chair, and a tripod chair newly made from old wood. Complementary accessories include a brightly colored serape, desert plants, pottery, and a folk-art snake.

The Eclectic Years

a broad range of styles popularized in the Victorian era

The many types of furniture made during the second half of the 19th century marked a new era in American design. From the 17th century to the early 1800s, only one style had dominated popular taste at any given time, but with the Victorians came diversity. Trends in decorating not only encompassed the comfortable and the practical, but also included the rustic, the exotic, the sentimental, and the eccentric.

While the machine age was making it possible for more people to afford more furniture, it was also causing a yearning for a "simpler time." Indeed, many of the furniture styles that became popular during the Victorian period were products of a nostalgic interest in the preindustrial past. Furniture made of animal horns, for example, was meant to recall the romance of the vanishing western frontier, and pieces in the Colonial Revival style celebrated a "lost" tradition of handcraftsmanship. Wood and cast-iron furnishings sprouting roots and leaves captured a sense of rustic simplicity. Yet while each popular furniture type was vastly different from the next, all shared in the romantic spirit of the time.

A twig rocker and table typify the eccentric designs of rustic wood furniture.

Wicker Furniture

The late-19th-century love seat at right is woven of reed; the set-in seat is made of pressed cane. Forming an elegant line, the gently rolled shape of the back and arms is a common design element in Victorian wicker.

Of the various furniture types that swept into fashion during the Victorian era, wicker—a catch-all term for furniture made of woven rattan, willow, rush, reed, cane, grasses, and paper fiber—was among the most widely favored. As likely to grace the parlor of a country cottage as it was to appear on the porch of a seaside hotel, wicker was appreciated for its light weight and comfort. It also gained great popularity as the result of a contemporary movement advocating "sanitary" living: the open weave not only made the versatile furniture easy to clean—a high priority—but also permitted air circulation, which was linked to good health.

Wicker was known in this country from colonial times, but it was not until the mid-19th century that the American wicker industry developed. In 1844, Cyrus Wakefield, an enterprising grocer from Boston, tried wrapping an old chair with rattan—then used as packing material on cargo ships from the Orient—that he found discarded on the city wharves. Recognizing the untapped potential of this flexible material, Wakefield soon left the grocery trade and became a rattan importer. The Wakefield Rattan Company, which manufactured wicker, was founded in South Reading, Massachusetts, in 1855.

In the early Victorian period, wicker furniture made by Wakefield and a growing number of competitors was fashioned from cane, the outer sheath of the rattan stem. Woven around hard-

Continued

*Clockwise from above
left: a turn-of-the-century
log holder; a rattan rocking
settee, also made around
1900; and a circa 1910 cane
chair complete with a book
rack, cup holder, and
retractable footrest.*

wood frames, the durable, water-resistant cane proved especially good for porch and garden furniture—mainly chairs, tables, and settees. Eventually, however, Wakefield discovered that the inner pith of rattan, known as reed, was also suitable for making wicker furniture. More pliant than cane, reed lent itself to the elaborate designs dictated by the Victorian taste for ornament. Reed furniture was deemed so attractive, in fact, that wicker soon became popular for indoor use: wicker suites were made for the parlor and bedroom, and accent pieces, such as magazine racks and plant stands, were used throughout the house.

The new, fashionable role of wicker as indoor furniture led to an even greater explosion of forms. In particular, there was a taste for specialized pieces such as vanities, fire screens, phonograph cabinets, easels, and tea carts. One of the most novel was the "posing chair," an extremely ornate seat designed to glamorize portrait sitters—especially children—and used exclusively as a photographers' prop.

As pieces were made in intricate patterns—spider webs and snowflakes were favorites—adornments grew increasingly complex. Ornate curlicues, beadwork, and arabesques were common embellishments, and "theme" chairs often incorporated woven motifs of stars, hearts, banjos, fans, and flags in their backs. Colorful reeds as well as satin ribbons were also sometimes woven in. Whereas cane was usually left natural

or lacquered—the shiny bark resists most finishes—reed furniture was generally stained or painted, often to match the decor of a room.

As changing tastes at the turn of the century called for simpler forms and more subtle decoration, wicker became more streamlined. To reduce costs, pieces were made with open latticework, which required less labor than tight weaving. At the same time, less expensive materials like prairie grass and paper fiber stiffened with glue began to replace rattan.

One entrepreneur, however, realized that the public still wanted tightly woven wicker—but at more reasonable prices. In 1917, Marshall Lloyd, a well-known inventor and maker of wicker baby carriages, perfected a mechanized loom for weaving paper fiber into flat, wickerlike sheets. These were then fitted onto separately made furniture frames. Lloyd's idea caught on, and by the 1920s, most American wicker furniture was made by the Lloyd process.

This plain, angular Lloyd loom furniture had such a strong influence on the wicker industry that even handmade rattan pieces were produced in designs that imitated Lloyd's machine-loomed styles. Wicker now featured boxy lines and gentle curves instead of sweeping scrolls, and a simple diamond design began to replace the more elaborate patterns. Many pieces were fitted with cushions of chintz or linen, as the more rigid machine-made pieces did not offer the comfortable "give" of earlier designs.

Many baby carriages, such as the circa 1908 example above left, were made of wicker because the woven material was easy to clean and considered hygienic. The early-1900s sewing basket above right was designed to fit into the corner of a room. Its upholstered top allowed it to double as a seat.

REPAIRING WICKER

If you own a piece of wicker furniture that is worn or damaged, don't feel you have to consign it to a yard sale or throw it away. Many procedures for mending wicker are easy to master and require only a basic understanding of wicker construction techniques and materials.

The broad family of wicker actually includes a number of different materials, including cane, reed, and machine-made paper fiber. It is fairly easy to distinguish among these common types: reed is usually round, cane is flat, and both have a straight, visible grain. Paper fiber is made of machine-twisted paper strands that look similar to string, often with a stiff wire core that provides added strength.

Most wicker furniture has three main elements: the frame, the spokes, and the weavers. The frame (usually made of wood) gives the piece its underlying shape and strength. The spokes (usually lengths of reed or paper fiber) serve as the framework around which the wicker is woven. The weavers, usually cane, reed, or paper fiber, are the lengths of material that are woven under and over the spokes.

Before you begin a repair, check your piece to see whether there are any serious problems. If there is structural damage, you should take the piece to a professional. Minor fraying, wear, and nonstructural breakage, however, are usually easy to fix yourself if you follow some general guidelines. As a rule, it is advisable not to use nails, which can rust; they can also pull out and damage the wicker. Gluing is also not recommended because most wicker fibers expand and contract with changing climatic conditions, causing glue to crack. The best repairs are those that involve tucking and wrapping the wicker material you are using so that it is held in place by tension alone.

You will find that replacement materials are readily available at craft shops and through mail order from craft supply houses. To be sure the material matches the original, care-fully snip off a small piece from the damaged area and use it as a sample. For cutting, you will need sharp, diagonal wire clippers, available at a hardware store.

When measuring replacement pieces, you will have to gauge the amount by eye, so be sure to give yourself plenty to work with; you can always cut off the excess when you have finished the repair. Cut the pieces on an angle; the pointed ends are easier to work into the weave. Some materials need to be soaked in water to become pliable enough to handle easily: soak cane for five minutes, and reed for ten minutes (but no longer). Never soak paper fiber, which will disintegrate.

The directions opposite are for correcting three of the most common wicker problems: loose wrapping, broken spokes, and damaged weaving. In each case, before you begin you will need to remove any damaged material, snipping carefully with diagonal cutters. If replacing a spoke, first determine whether the spoke is structural. The spokes on a wicker piece are usually found in openwork sections located between two bands of weaving. If the end of the spoke is continued as part of the weaving in the band, it is structural and its repair should be left to an expert. If the spoke is not woven into the band, you can remove it safely.

REWRAPPING A LEG

◆ Cut a piece of replacement material and make a perpendicular fold to create a one-inch tab at one end. Place fold on inside of leg, tab side down, at right angles to direction of wrapping, and hold in place with thumb (Illustration 1); wrap material snugly around leg, winding over tab to secure it. Continue wrapping until leg is covered. To finish, leave last two rounds of wrapping loose; after last wrap, feed end of material under loose rounds on inside of leg (Illustration 2). Pull end to tighten and lock end of material in place. Snip end flush with wrapping.

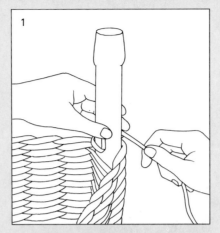
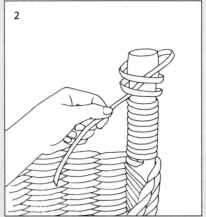

REPLACING SPOKES

◆ With diagonal cutters, snip off damaged spoke at bottom edge of upper band of weaving (Illustration 1) and at top edge of bottom band, leaving about ¾ inch projecting. Thread one end of replacement spoke into bottom band alongside cut-off end of damaged spoke. Gauge length of spoke to bottom edge of top weaving, add about two inches, and snip. Carefully work upper end of spoke up into weaving alongside cut-off end of damaged spoke (Illustration 2). Tension will hold new spoke in place.

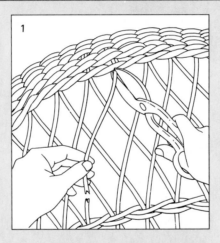
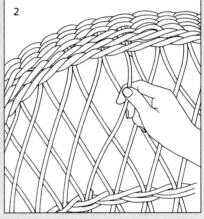

REWEAVING

◆ Starting at upper edge of gap to be filled, trim each broken weaver so that end passes under a spoke and one inch beyond. Place end of replacement weaver one inch under spoke, alongside old weaver and in opposite direction (Illustration 1). With one hand, hold end of new weaver in place; with other hand, run free end of weaver under and over spokes (Illustration 2). At end of row, run end under a spoke and snip off, leaving one-inch end to hold weaver in place. Repeat for each weaver to be replaced until gap is filled.

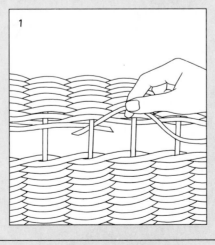
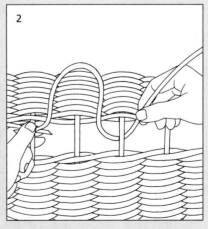

Cast-Iron Furniture

Clockwise from near right: a Victorian cast-iron hall tree featuring curvilinear and floral forms; a circa 1870 garden chair, with "animal paw" feet and a leafy, filigreed back; and a circa 1865 garden chair made in the grapevine pattern, which was particularly popular in the Victorian period.

Introduced to the American public around 1840, the earliest cast-iron furniture was made by foundries specializing in architectural ironwork. Unlike wrought iron, which is heated in a forge and hammered by hand, cast iron is made by pouring molten metal into molds, a process that makes it easier to create fluid and intricate shapes. It was logical that the same technology that was already yielding elaborate columns, fences, and gates could also be used to mass-produce furnishings for the home and garden. Individual furniture parts were turned out from molds, then assembled and bolted together into completed pieces.

The first cast-iron furniture in America was made for outdoor use in parks, cemeteries, and gardens. The casting process permitted all manner of organic forms, which made the furniture particularly suited to the romantic or "picturesque" garden that was popular during much of the 1800s. Designed to blend in with the natural, wild look of these gardens, the chairs, tables, and settees—usually painted green—sprouted iron grapevines, ferns, and morning-glories. In the same spirit, pieces grew gnarled-root feet and branches in imitation of the rustic wood furniture that was also in vogue during the Victorian period.

Around 1850, cast-iron furniture for indoor use was introduced. The designs imitated those of wooden furniture in a variety of Victorian styles, and the pieces were usually painted black or bronze. One especially popular furnishing for the home was the hat-and-umbrella stand, which, fitted with hooks for hanging coats, bonnets, umbrellas, and walking sticks, was placed in the foyer. Like cast-iron garden pieces, these "hall trees" also featured such appropriate embellishments as branches and leaves, and were often fitted with mirrors.

The circa 1875 garden settee above is distinguished by an elegant fern-frond pattern. Although cast-iron benches could hardly be considered comfortable, seating pieces were nevertheless the most common furniture forms.

The rustic bentwood bench, top, is typical of the pieces crafted by rural woodsmen. The simpler settee,

bottom, was made by the Old Hickory Chair Company of Martinsville, Indiana, around 1902.

Rustic Wood Furniture

Rustic wood furnishings made of roots, branches, and bark were especially popular in England's romantic gardens at the end of the 18th century, and by the 1840s the fashion for these idiosyncratic pieces had reached America.

The rustic tradition coincided with the popular Victorian notion that the good life was to be found in nature and simplicity. At the time, the taming of the American wilderness had begun and the industrial age was fast approaching. In response to encroaching civilization, urban parks, suburban gardens, and rustic summer retreats were becoming fixtures on the American landscape. Rather than a force to be feared, nature was now perceived as a "country parlor" to be enjoyed. Rustic furniture was the perfect appointment for this vast outdoor room.

The wood used to make rustic furniture—typically ash, elm, birch, cedar, hickory, and spruce—was left as close as possible to its natural state and pieces often incorporated tree stumps, whole branches, and gnarled roots. Any irregularities, such as knots, forks, and burls only added to the effect. Even the finish was "natural": instead of paint or varnish, rustic furniture

The rocking chair above left, made in the early 1900s, features a combination of bent saplings and slats. In typical rustic tradition, the design of the stick-style plant stand above right was inspired by the natural forms of the tree branches— complete with bark— used to craft it.

Continued

101

*Made for an Adirondack mountain camp by Ernest Stowe, a well-known craftsman, this circa 1900
sideboard shows a traditional furniture form adapted in rustic materials.*

might be decorated with a veneer of white-birch bark or mosaic patterns composed of tiny twigs. Among the many types that were made, the best known is probably stick furniture, characterized by branches tied or nailed together to create simple, functional forms. Another common type is bentwood, in which flexible pieces of wood were literally bent to make fancy chairs, settees, and rockers.

Rustic pieces included porch and garden furnishings as well as beds, dressers, sideboards, desks, dining tables, clocks, and lamps designed for the interiors of summer lodges and cabins. Much of this furniture was crafted in the regions where the wilderness resorts and "great camps" were located. Among these areas were Minne-

sota's lake country, northern New England, Appalachia, northern Michigan, and the Adirondack region of New York State, a primary center for rustic furniture making.

Some of the best rustic pieces were made during the winter by the guides, trappers, and handymen who worked at the summer camps. Rustic furniture was also mass-produced by factories. Most prominent among the manufacturers was the Old Hickory Chair Company of Martinsville, Indiana, which shipped quantities of its durable hickory-sapling chairs, settees, and swings to hotels and camps between the 1890s and 1940s. Although factory-made, this furniture had the same rough quality as the pieces that were handcrafted.

The early-20th-century rustic wood pieces above display the two most prevalent types of rustic decoration. The desk, left, features a "veneer" of white-birch bark, a light, decorative bark favored for interior furnishings. The mosaic work that trims the top of the table, right, was executed in twigs.

THE GREAT CAMPS

Today "roughing it" brings to mind images of tents and camp stoves, but in the decades between the 1870s and the 1930s, the phrase meant something quite different to many of America's wealthy citizens.

Families such as the Morgans, Astors, Vanderbilts, and Posts customarily spent part of each year roughing it at one of their privately owned "great camps" in the Adirondack Mountain region of New York State. A typical camp consisted of a main lodge with a spacious porch, as well as a separate kitchen and dining hall, "sleeping cabin," and guest cabin. In at least one camp there was also a bowling alley.

Most camps lacked hot water and central heating, but they all had plenty of servants. In peak season, the staff at Sagamore, Alfred G. Vanderbilt's camp, numbered forty. In the 1922 edition of her *Etiquette*, Emily Post advised camp guests not to be put off if the butler wore hunting clothes and moccasins.

Featuring spacious interiors where branches grew out of ceiling beams and birch bark might serve as wallpaper, the stone and log camps were generally built by the same craftsmen who fashioned their rustic furnishings. Here, in this fantasy setting, it was possible for city dwellers to escape civilization and enjoy nature in relative comfort.

"Campers" relax on the porch at Trophy Lodge, c. 1890.

Echo Point Camp, right, built in 1883 by the governor of Connecticut.

The "Living Room Cabin" of Kamp Kill Kare, c. 1916.

George Wilson, A.G. Vanderbilt's gardener, making a rustic table.

The porch columns on the lodge boasted tree-stump capitals.

A stuffed owl perches on the headboard of the rustic bed above.

A young woman poses on a rustic bench draped with a fur pelt.

A comfortable hammock, above, was an essential porch furnishing.

Typical camp decorations included American Indian artifacts.

Horn
Furniture

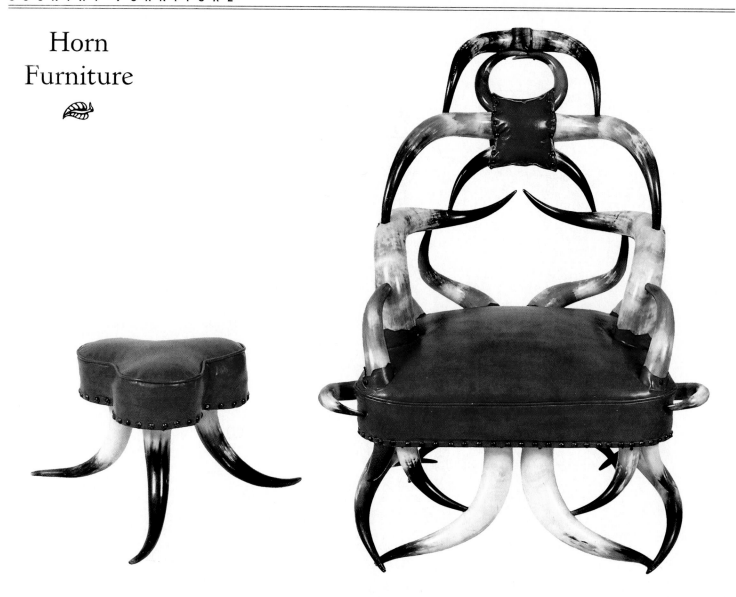

The matching armchair and stool above were made around the turn of the century from the horns of longhorn steers.

Inspired by the romance of the vanishing western frontier, horn furniture was popular in America from the end of the 1800s through the early 1900s. By the late 19th century, the Victorians had already developed a taste for oddities that coincided with a growing nostalgia for frontier life. The result was a vogue for decorating with such American exotica as buffalo heads, bearskin rugs, and furniture featuring various animal parts, including horns from steer, antelope, and buffalo, and antlers from moose, stag, and elk.

Horn furniture was designed for the libraries, billiards rooms, and smoking dens of fashionable eastern gentlemen, and for the rustic summer camps they frequented. The most common forms included tables, stools, settees, armchairs, rockers, hatracks, and hall stands. Incongruously, some of the seating pieces were upholstered with fringe-trimmed silk or damask, but most were covered in more appropriate materials such as prairie dog hide and sheepskin.

While horn furniture is often associated with the West, little of it was actually used there, but instead was made for sale back East. Texas, with its plentiful supply of longhorn cattle, was one center of horn furniture making. Curiously, however, some of the best pieces came from Austria and Germany, where such furniture had been popular earlier in the 1800s.

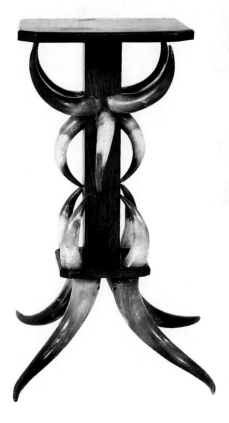

The circa 1890 hall stand above left boasts thirty-two horns and was created by Wenzel Friedrich,
a well-known Texas furniture maker. The plant stand above right is made of horn, mahogany, and oak.

The circa 1867 bed above features three of the decorative techniques that characterize Cottage furniture: grain-painting— here imitating oak— stenciled fruit motifs, and painted scrolls.

Cottage furniture was first produced around the mid-1800s and remained popular until the 1920s. Designed for simple country cottages, the inexpensive factory-made pieces—painted with gay floral motifs or decorated with spool turnings—were specifically meant to appeal to the tastes and pocketbooks of a new middle-class market. However, the extremely popular Cottage furniture was also used by the well-to-do, usually in their smaller bedrooms or servants' quarters, or in their summer residences.

The fashion for Cottage furniture was encouraged by important tastemakers of the era. Beginning in 1849, *Godey's Lady's Book,* then the most influential women's magazine in America, ran an illustrated monthly column on the style entitled "Cottage Furniture Department."

The greatest proponent of Cottage furniture, however, was Andrew Jackson Downing, a lead-

Cottage Furniture

ing 19th-century American designer and landscape architect. A champion of fresh air and country living, Downing was the author of several books, including *Cottage Residences* (1842) and *The Architecture of Country Houses* (1850), in which he introduced designs for picturesque, romantic cottages that blended with their natural environment. The wholesome suburbs Downing envisioned for the workingman and his family would offer relief from congested cities and be-

come the setting for domestic harmony. To decorate these unpretentious cottages, Downing called for "chaste, simple, and expressive" furniture that was also durable and comfortable.

Cottage furniture was used primarily in the bedroom, which by the Victorian era had become a feminine domain. For the first time, bedrooms were decorated with as much consideration for appearance as for comfort and convenience. Women demanded pretty, grace-

Continued

Cottage furniture, often painted in pastel colors, was sold in suites for the bedroom that might include such pieces as the mirrored dressing table above left and the circa 1881 commode above right.

Beds like the one above were among the most popular forms of spool furniture. Other spool-turned bed styles included the low "hired man's" bed, the tester bed, and the day bed.

ful bedroom furnishings and manufacturers responded with suites of painted pieces that included beds, chests of drawers, washstands, dressing tables, and towel racks. Eventually, sofas and chairs were added to these suites. Prices for a full set of Cottage furniture ranged from about $21 to $250.

In effect, such furniture was a less ornate and lower-priced version of the formal Rococo, Gothic, and Renaissance Revival styles in vogue during the same period, but it was considered just as stylish. Instead of costly carving, Cottage pieces were decorated with paint, applied moldings, or machine-made "spool" turnings; some pieces featured all three ornamental techniques.

The decoratively painted furniture was usually offered in black or white, or light muted colors such as lilac, powder blue, green, and gray, and generally had a hard enamel finish. These pieces were characteristically embellished with graining, floral and fruit motifs, scrolls, crests, medallions, striping, and scenic vignettes. Designs were often stenciled rather than painted freehand. Most pieces were manufactured in less expensive softwoods such as pine, poplar and birch, although some hardwoods—maple, cherry, ash, hickory, and walnut—were occasionally used, sometimes in combination with softwoods. Construction methods were geared to keeping down costs: the case of a chest, for instance, was generally put together with glue or dowels rather than dovetail joints.

The pieces with spool-turned decoration were also known as Elizabethan Revival furniture although they more accurately recalled the heavily turned pieces of the English Restoration of the mid- to late 1600s. In addition to spool shapes, the stylized turnings of the American pieces featured bobbin, spiral, knot, button, sausage, and vase-and-ring shapes. Such turnings were used to make chair uprights, bed spindles and posts, and table legs and trestles. Split in half lengthwise, turnings were also affixed to flat surfaces such as chest fronts to imitate hand carving. The demand for spool furniture was so great that factories using the multiblade lathe originally engineered for making wooden thread spools often found it more profitable to sell their spool stock to furniture makers instead of to textile companies.

Because the legendary songstress Jenny Lind supposedly slept in a low-post spool bed, that form became particularly popular, and in time all spool furniture became known as the Jenny Lind style. The most common spool pieces in the bedroom besides beds were tables, washstands, and towel racks. Other spool pieces such as sofas, chairs, ottomans, whatnots, and tables—especially sets of nesting tables—were designed for drawing rooms, libraries, and parlors. Stands and tables were made suitable for these more formal settings by the use of fine hardwoods, including rosewood and mahogany, and the addition of slate or marble tops.

The circa 1850 spool-legged mahogany table above left was probably made for use in the parlor, while the less formal grain-painted cradle above right is typical of Cottage pieces designed for a child's bedroom.

Colonial Revival

The Centennial Exposition held in Philadelphia in 1876 touched off a nationwide interest in America's colonial heritage. For the first time, furniture and other decorative arts from 18th-century America were appreciated as antiques, and also inspired a market for new "colonial" furniture.

Victorian furniture manufacturers, quick to take advantage of the general trend toward historical design, had already begun producing a series of "revivals" as early as the 1840s. So pervasive was the nostalgia that an 1884 furniture-trade publication reported, "The manufacture of antiques has become a modern industry."

Emerging in the 1870s, the Colonial Revival style followed the flurry of European revivals that included the Gothic, Rococo, Renaissance, and Elizabethan. But unlike the furniture made in those revival styles, Colonial Revival pieces reproduced the furniture made in early America. Meant to evoke simpler days, revive a handcrafted look, and provide "instant ancestry" for this nation of immigrants, the colonial revival flourished, and the furniture is still made today.

Popular forms included rockers, settees, gate-leg tables, high chests, low chests, block-front chests of drawers, and a range of Windsor chairs. While some pieces were faithful copies of colonial designs, others were loose interpretations. A famous Colonial Revival dressing table used by Mrs. Woodrow Wilson in the White House, for instance, simultaneously combined Chippendale, Sheraton, Hepplewhite, and Empire elements. Manufacturers also produced a number of novelties meant to recall the good old days, including a "spinning wheel" chair, which was made with an old flax wheel for its backrest.

Many of the manufacturing concerns that produced these pieces for a middle-class market were located in the growing cities of the Midwest. Grand Rapids, in particular, was an ideal location for the new mechanized furniture factories: the city had not only a skilled immigrant labor pool but also plentiful supplies of lumber and water, and good railroad connections. Known as "Furniture City," Grand Rapids had become home to more than thirty furniture manufacturers by the turn of the century.

These two factory-made chairs display a combination of styles typical of Colonial Revival pieces. The early-1900s chair above left has Queen Anne and William and Mary details; the circa 1930 chair above right is a hybrid of Queen Anne and Chippendale styles.

Simple Country Furnishings

*timeless, practical pieces with
an inherent appeal*

Favorites among collectors today are the country furnishings known variously as "primitive," "rural," "rustic," or "folk." Whatever the name, these basic pieces—including such familiar forms as settles, farm tables, dry sinks, and slat-back chairs—are characterized by a distance from mainstream design and a simplicity of workmanship. Reduced to bare essentials, they show no overt stylistic influence and are generally stripped of any ornament that might take extra time, materials, money, or effort to produce.

Made until the early 1900s, the simple country furniture shown in this chapter includes pieces that were commonly used by city and country dwellers alike. It was produced in factories, by trained woodworkers catering to homeowners' specific needs, and by self-sufficient individuals who were furnishing their own homes as inexpensively as possible. The quality of craftsmanship is quite varied, yet almost all of these well-worn pieces embody a certain character that has come with age and use.

The appeal of this simple 1800s cupboard derives from its timeworn look.

Seating Furniture

Typical seating furniture in the country household included such sturdy, serviceable pieces as stools, rocking chairs, wagon seats, and settles. Stools are among the oldest type of seating furniture made by European settlers in this country. They were used for such tasks as milking and hearth cooking, and tall ones could double as tables. The simplest stools were nothing more than shaped, crosscut log seats fitted with hewn legs. A more refined form was the joint, or joined, stool, often consisting of turned parts.

Rocking chairs were first used in the colonies in the mid-1700s. Early examples were made simply by adding rockers to existing chairs, but by the early 1800s, rockers had become an integral part of chair design.

A kind of double chair, short-legged wagon seats—made from about 1790 to 1860—served as seating in wagons, but were also commonly removed for use in homes or in meetinghouses. Such pieces are often worn on the sides from being moved in and out of wagons.

Settles were common in America from the 1600s to the 1800s. Designed to provide protection from drafts and hold in the warmth of the fire, these high-backed benches were used near the hearth. Some had storage seats fitted with drawers or lift-up tops.

Clockwise from top left: a circa 1700 cypress joint stool; a pine milking stool; an early 1800s New England rocking chair with red paint; and a circa 1825 walnut stool from Ohio.

The wagon bench above, with a woven splint seat, dates from the early 1800s and is thought to be from Pennsylvania. The pine settle at left, still bearing its original red paint, was made in New England around 1820.

Country Tables

The trestle table, top left, and the sawbuck table, top right, are both pine pieces dating from the 1700s. Made with simple board tops, the two table types are closely related.

The table was made in a greater variety of styles than any other furniture form. The most basic type is the trestle table, commonly used in this country from about 1650 to 1840. Little changed from its medieval prototype—a removable board set on supports—a trestle table consisted of a plank top supported on I-shaped "trestles," or uprights, stabilized with a stretcher bar. When not in use, the table could easily be dismantled and put out of the

way. Tops on early pieces often measure as long as twelve feet; many 19th-century tables were generally only half that length.

The sawbuck table is similar to the trestle table, but instead of trestles, it has crossed legs that resemble those of a sawhorse, or sawbuck. On some sawbuck tables, the stretchers bracing the crossed legs were placed at a height convenient for use as footrests; two more braces might be added under the top to form a storage well.

Another type of large table, now called a harvest table, featured a long, narrow top that could be expanded by one or two wide drop leaves supported on slides or brackets.

The huntboard, or slab, is a table form characterized by long legs and a board top. Unique to the South, huntboards were made from the late 1700s through the 1800s. They are usually forty to fifty inches high—taller than the average table—and it is believed that they were designed

to be used by diners who ate while standing. Some huntboards were placed on the porch, perhaps to serve riders after a hunt; others, made of fine hardwoods, were designed for use in the dining room.

A more versatile serving table is the semicircular table, which could be pushed against a wall. Low examples were sometimes joined to form a small, round dining table or were used as extensions for a square table.

The 1830s huntboard, bottom left, is from Georgia. Simple pine tables were often decorated with paint, as on the late-1700s harvest table, bottom center, and the 1880s side table, bottom right.

MAKING A COUNTRY BENCH

Making your own country furniture can be a rewarding experience. A small, simple piece like the bench above requires no special woodworking skills or equipment. For this project you will need only basic household carpentry tools and inexpensive pine boards, which you can have cut to the proper length at a lumberyard.

You can simply finish the bench with a plain coat of varnish, or you might try a decorative paint treatment like graining or the sponge-painting technique shown here. For a long-lasting finish, it is a good idea to protect the paint or varnish with polyurethane.

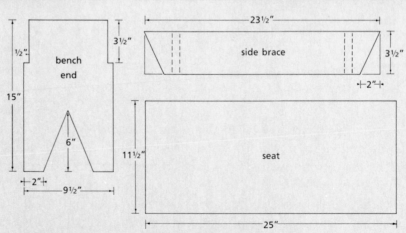

NOTE: *Boards are sold in stock sizes: for example, 1 x 10, 1 x 4, 1 x 12. The actual measurements of such boards are approximately ¼ inch smaller in thickness and ½ inch smaller in width, thus a 1 x 10 is really ¾ x 9½ inches. The widths given above reflect the actual measurements of stock-size boards.*

MATERIALS

· Two 1 x 10 #2 pine boards, each 15 inches long ·
· Two 1 x 4 #2 pine boards, each 23½ inches long ·
· One 1 x 12 #2 pine board, 25 inches long ·
· #4d finishing nails · Small-size countersink nail set ·
· Hammer · L-square · Pencil · Yardstick ·
· Hand coping saw or saber saw · 1-inch brush ·
· Wood glue · Wood putty · Sandpaper ·
· Varnish or paint, for finish ·

DIRECTIONS

1. To make bench ends, use 1 x 10 boards. You will make one bench end first and use it as template for other end. To make cutouts in top of bench end, measure and draw ½ x 3½-inch rectangle at each corner of one end of board; use L-square to ensure 90° angles. To make notch that will form legs at other end of board, measure in from corners to find center point and mark with dot. Measure up 6 inches from center point to locate top of triangle and mark with dot. Measure in 2 inches from each corner along bottom of board to locate bottom corners of triangle and mark with dots.

2. Using yardstick, connect three dots with pencil to form triangle. With coping saw or saber saw, make all three cutouts; sand edges lightly, being sure not to round off corners. Using first board as template, trace shapes of three notches on second board. Cut and sand.

3. To make side braces, use 1 x 4 boards. On long side of one board, measure 2 inches in from bottom right corner and mark. Using yardstick, draw straight line from mark to top right corner to make angle. Repeat in reverse for left side. With coping saw or saber saw, cut along lines. Sand lightly, being sure not to round off corners. Using first board as template, trace angles onto second board. Cut and sand as above. To make guidelines for assembly, on each side brace measure in ¾ inch from new corners along bottom and mark. Measure in 1½ inches from same corners and mark. Using yardstick, draw perpendicular lines across board at each mark. Flip board over and repeat process for guidelines on opposite side.

4. To make seat, use 1 x 12 board. Sand all corners thoroughly so that they are smooth and rounded.

5. To assemble bench, brush glue on inside edges of rectangular cutouts in tops of one bench end. Brush glue between parallel guide lines on one side of a side brace. Using parallel guide lines on opposite side of side brace as sight lines, press side brace into cutouts (Illustration A). While glue is still wet, use L-square to make sure corners and bench ends are square. Hammer nails through side braces into end boards before glue sets, placing three nails at even intervals between parallel sight lines (Illustration B). Wipe off excess glue. Repeat process for second side brace.

6. Brush glue along top edges of end boards and side braces, and center seat in position on top. At even intervals on each side of top, hammer six nails through seat into tops of side braces (Illustration C). Wipe off excess glue, and countersink nails about ¹⁄₁₆ inch below seat surface, using small-size countersink nail set. Fill nail holes with wood putty. Let dry and sand smooth. Sand edges and surfaces, and finish with varnish or paint.

A
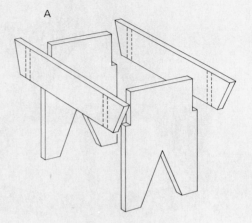

B
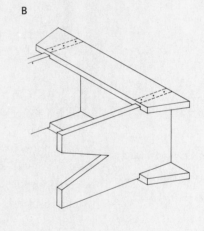

C
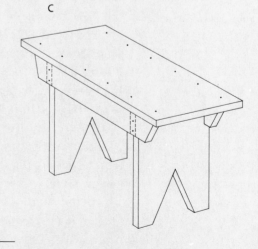

Stands and Dry Sinks

Semicircular or "demilune" stepped shelves, such as the late-19th-century set above left, were usually painted; green was the favored color. The 19th-century bucket bench above right was used to hold full water buckets; its bottom shelf is braced for strength.

Bucket benches, dry sinks, and stands were among the most common of furnishings in the country household. The bucket bench, or water bench, was designed to hold buckets filled from a well or hand pump. Made from the 1700s until the late 1800s, it was usually found in the kitchen, entryway, or washroom, or out on the back porch. Heavy buckets were stored on the bottom shelf, which was built at a convenient height to make lifting easier. The top shelf was handy for storing dippers, soap, towels, washbasins, and water pitchers. Bucket benches were also used on washday to hold tubs of water and such laundry equipment as washboards and clothes forks.

The dry sink, or washbench, served as a washtub. Early dry sinks were only slightly more elaborate than bucket benches: a wooden trough simply replaced an upper shelf. Water was poured into the trough from a pitcher or bucket. (Later dry sinks, made to resemble cupboards, were serviced by hand pumps or faucets.) The wooden "sink," or well, was lined with zinc, tin, or enamel; a cork or corncob served as a drain stopper. Washpans, as well as soap and linens, were stored behind doors on the shelves below. When a woman was finished washing fruits, vegetables, flowerpots, clothing, dishes—or her children—in the sink, the water was drained into a pail or through a pipe to the outdoors.

Equally functional, but more decorative, were semicircular stepped shelves. Used to display potted plants or vases of cut flowers, such shelves were found on porches or in solariums in Victorian homes, and in flower shops. They were also commonly used for displaying summer produce sold by the roadside.

All of these furniture forms were usually made of inexpensive wood, such as pine, and then painted to help preserve the wood and protect it from water stains and dry rot. Because such pieces were often built with hard use in mind, they can be rather crude in construction.

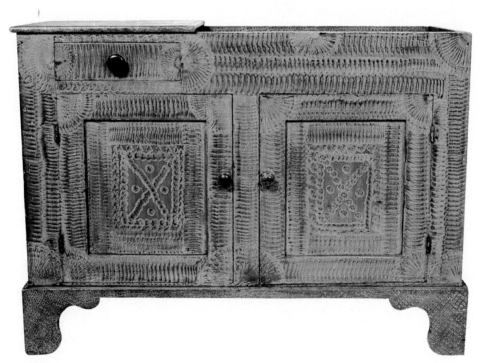

*Clockwise from top left: a simple tablelike dry sink with an unlined trough; a single-door
dry sink of the type used throughout the 19th century; and a double-door dry sink fitted
with a single drawer and decorated with grain-painting.*

Clockwise from top left: a dough box, or kneading table, set on a stand; a circa 1717 livery cupboard made of pine with oak spindles; and a circa 1710 pine food cupboard with a paneled door.

Food Storage

Before iceboxes became common around the turn of the 19th century, specialized cupboards were necessary to store food. One type, the livery cupboard, is mentioned in New England inventories as early as 1655. Made to be built-in, freestanding, or mounted on a wall, such cupboards were fitted with pierced panels or wooden or wicker grills for ventilation. Following a medieval tradition, they were set at bedside to keep "liveries," or servings of food and drink, on hand at night.

A descendant of the livery cupboard is the safe—also called the meat safe, food safe, tin closet, or pie safe—which was widely used during the 1800s. Safes were fitted with pierced-tin panels, screens, wooden grills, or fabric to per-

mit air circulation and keep out insects. ("If ants are troublesome," advised Catharine Beecher in an 1869 issue of *The American Woman's Home*, "set the legs in tin cups of water.") Kept in a cool place, such as the cellar, safes were used to store baked goods, meats, and dairy products.

Other food storage pieces included jelly or jam cupboards, where preserves were commonly stored, and smaller multidrawer cupboards that could be set on a tabletop or hung on a wall.

A piece used for both the preparation and storage of food was the dough box, or kneading table, a portable trough often placed on a sturdy, splay-legged stand. After the dough was kneaded on the box top, the box was moved to a warm area and the dough placed inside to rise.

The mid-19th-century food safe above left, from Virginia, displays finely decorated door panels of painted tin. The twenty-inch-high tabletop cupboard above right was probably used to store spices and utensils.

THE VERSATILE HOOSIER

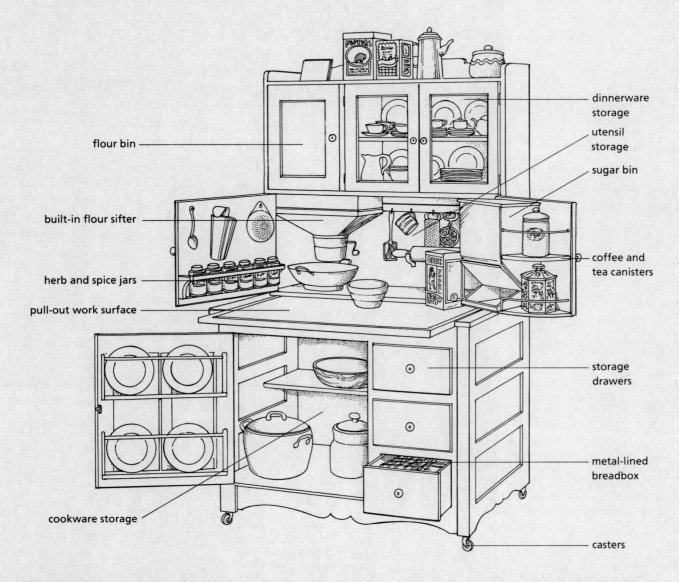

flour bin

built-in flour sifter

herb and spice jars

pull-out work surface

cookware storage

dinnerware storage

utensil storage

sugar bin

coffee and tea canisters

storage drawers

metal-lined breadbox

casters

The Hoosier Manufacturing company of New Castle, Indiana, called it "The silent servant with a hundred hands." A deluxe model cost about $19. But for $5 down and an additional $5 monthly, an up-to-date housewife in the early decades of the 1900s could enjoy the newest in kitchen furnishings: the timesaving, multipurpose kitchen cabinet.

The Hoosier Company was just one of the many firms to produce these cabinets from about 1900 to 1930. But because so many makers—including the Showers Brothers Company and the Sellers Company—were located in Indiana, all such kitchen cabinets have become known as hoosiers.

Set on casters, these centralized work centers represented the ultimate in convenience. Not only did they have an easy-to-clean work surface, but many also came with such options as a swing-out sugar container, a flour bin complete with sifter, moistureproof canisters, and even a menu planner.

Made of maple, pine, oak, or walnut, hoosiers had a natural finish or were enamel-painted—white, gray, blue, and apple green were popular colors. The work surfaces of earlier models were made of wood or a nickel and steel alloy. Later models had a porcelain-enameled counter.

Closed-door cupboards like the circa 1820 Ohio example at right are also called blind cupboards. This piece features its original green and red paint and brass hardware.

Country Cupboards

The progenitor of the cupboard as we know it today, the "cup board" appeared in America in the mid-1600s; the name originally referred to open board shelves that held cups and other dishware. By the end of the century, the shelves began to be encased in a frame and doors were added. In general, most cupboards consisted of an upper section, fitted with three or four shelves that might be enclosed by doors or left open, and a lower section that frequently contained drawers and cabinets. Either type of cupboard could be built-in or freestanding, but freestanding cupboards were usually made in two parts so that they could be disassembled and moved easily.

As parlors came to be more common in houses during the 18th century, the wedge-shaped corner cupboard became popular for this "best room." Here—following the fashionable English custom—it was used to display china and porcelain. Considered part of the woodwork in a room, built-in corner cupboards were often constructed with cornice moldings and baseboards and were painted to blend with the decor. While they had a top and bottom section, these space-saving cupboards were generally built as one piece. They had no feet, but sat directly on the floor.

Open-top cupboards, also known as Welsh dressers, hutches, or pewter cupboards, were de-

Continued

The 19th-century glass-door corner cupboard at left, of pine with walnut veneer, is from Texas.

129

The New England pine corner cupboard above left, made in the 1700s, features grooved shelves to hold plates.

rived from a similar European form. The upper shelves were usually stepped back, so that the top of the lower cupboard could be used as a counter. Here food was "dressed," or prepared for serving at the table. The top and shelves of such dressers were sometimes decoratively scalloped, which helped relieve their massive appearance.

Glass-door cupboards appeared in the mid-1800s, when glass became more readily available. New glass doors were frequently added to older dressers to keep the upper shelves free

from dust and dirt. As in a window, the glass panes were held in place by narrow strips of wood, or muntins; the horizontal muntins were usually aligned with the shelves, so that the contents of the cupboard, but not the shelves themselves, were visible. Such cupboards were occasionally used to store food, but primarily held pottery, glassware, tableware, and cooking utensils. Once sets of fine dishes and cutlery were accumulated, they were proudly displayed on the upper shelves, which were generally grooved and notched to hold the pieces securely.

The circa 1750 dresser above center and the double-door cupboard above right are both made of pine.

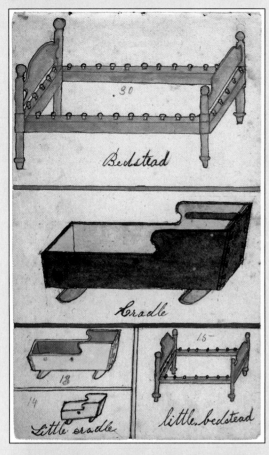

Bedstead

Cradle

13

14

Little cradle

15

little bedstead

No 4

burean

Washbench

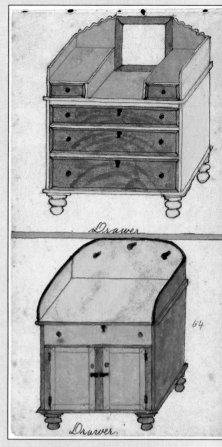

Drawer

64

Drawer.

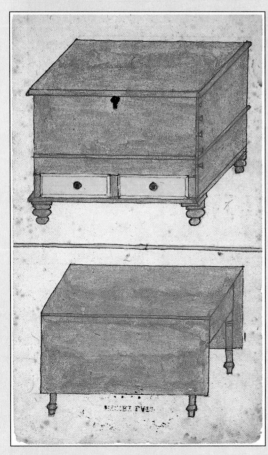

7

2

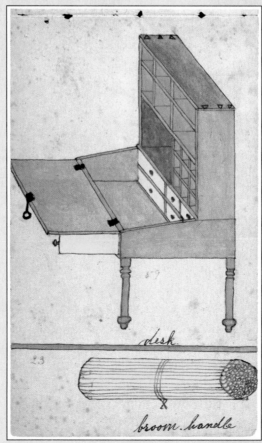

desk

23

broom handle

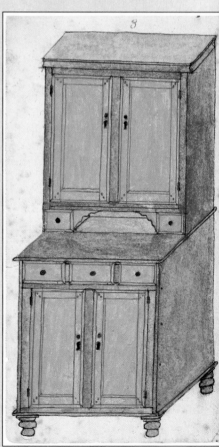

8

drawer

bench   bench

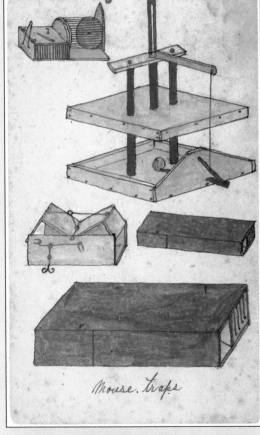

Mouse Traps

FROM A CRAFTSMAN'S HANDBOOK

Of the hundreds of craftsmen who supplied country households with their rudimentary, practical furnishings during the 18th and 19th centuries, most have remained anonymous. One whose name and work is known today, however, is Henry Lapp, a Pennsylvania Amish hardware merchant, carpenter, and cabinetmaker. Although a fine craftsman, Lapp is recalled not so much for his furniture—only a few pieces are extant—but for his illustrated handbook of goods for sale, now preserved at the Philadelphia Museum of Art.

Born in 1862 in the prosperous farm belt of Lancaster County, the enterprising Lapp established his business in 1898 on the main road to Philadelphia. Because he was deaf and partially mute, his pocket-size handbook must have been the means through which Lapp both communicated with his customers and advertised his products. In this simple, store-bought notebook, he depicted in pencil and watercolor a wide range of items that he either made or stocked for sale. These included furniture, farm equipment, and household articles: cupboards, settles, cradles, and desks; wagons, sleighs, and wheelbarrows; eggbeaters, bread toasters, toys, and mousetraps.

More than a mere catalog of wares, however, Henry Lapp's handbook is a record of the lifestyles and tastes of 19th-century rural Pennsylvanians. It shows furniture that is invariably plain and sturdy—the utilitarian chests, benches, and tables that appealed to the simple, industrious farm families of the region. Yet while such traditional Germanic forms as dower chests and wall boxes are represented, Lapp chose not to decorate these pieces with typical motifs such as unicorns and tulips. Instead, his furniture is plain, painted with the bright, solid colors preferred by the Welsh and Scotch-Irish settlers who lived in neighboring areas. It is not surprising that Lapp's work shows such a diversity of cultural influences. He often traveled the sixty miles east to Philadelphia for supplies, and would have been exposed to a variety of furniture forms and decorative techniques not used in his own community.

Lapp died in 1904, and his belongings were sold at auction soon after. It was not until the 1950s that his well-worn handbook, long forgotten, was discovered in the drawer of an old chest.

Shown at left are eight illustrated pages from the handbook of Henry Lapp, a late-19th-century Pennsylvania carpenter and cabinetmaker.

The Federal Revival style wardrobe at right, a Victorian piece, was made around 1870. Crafted of inexpensive softwoods, such large case pieces were often painted or sponged to suggest the look of fine-grained hardwoods.

Bedroom Furniture

Wardrobes, commode chests, and washstands were among the personal furnishings found in the bedroom. Fitted inside with shelves and pegs, a wardrobe was often used to keep clothing and linens for the entire family, and there was usually a drawer under the doors for extra storage. Because wardrobes were so large—frequently over six feet tall—they were generally constructed in sections so that they could be taken apart and moved relatively easily.

Before indoor plumbing became relatively common in the late 1800s, washstands and commodes were absolute necessities in the bedroom. Washstands were tall, two-tiered tables that fea-tured an upper shelf with a hole cut in it to accommodate a basin and pitcher. A lower shelf or drawers held a chamber set, which included a soap dish, toothbrush cup, and shaving mug.

Commode chests or commode washstands were case pieces that served the same purpose as the simpler, table-type washstand. The commode consisted of a top section that was built like a chest with a lift-up top. The deep well inside was used as a washstand, where a basin and pitcher were kept. A drawer beneath the well stored a razor, a soap dish, and towels. A bottom section featured a cupboard, in which the lidded "slop jar" (used to hold dirty wash water) and the chamber pot were stored.

These two mid-19th-century commodes show different designs that were popular in that period. The pine piece above left features scrolled legs, while the simpler piece above right is grain-painted. Both pieces could have been made in a factory or in a cabinet-maker's shop.

Children's Furniture

Furniture was made for children in America from the earliest days of the colonies. While there were some chests, tables, and stools made as miniature versions of adult furniture, most small-scale furnishings were designed specifically to suit the needs of children. This furniture included highchairs and potty chairs, as well as "standing stools," or "walking cages," which were similar in function to the modern wheeled walkers that are used to help teach toddlers to walk.

Cradles, made of wicker or wood, were among the first furniture forms in America. Early wooden cradles were simple—no more than a box fitted with a pair of rockers. Such pieces typically had high headboards and footboards, and sometimes a hood to help provide protection from drafts; later examples were raised off the floor on swinging frames. Cradles generally had solid wooden sides, but one type of mid-18th-century cradle—developed by a Windsor chair maker and consequently known as a Windsor cradle—featured turned spindles.

The most common type of children's beds were trundle beds (there were fancy four-posters similar to those made for adults, but they were rare). The simplest beds, however, were just open boxes set on block legs; these were fitted with the same type of roping used on full-size beds as mattress supports.

Like some cradles, highchairs and small children's chairs were custom made in many of the popular furniture styles, including Queen Anne and Chippendale, and by the 19th century were being produced by such manufacturers as the Hitchcock Factory in Barkhamsted, Connecticut. Simpler homemade chairs might have slat backs and woven seats of splint or hide. One very modest type of highchair had a high back and side "wings" to shield the occupant from drafts, and a well with a plank seat to hold the child snugly. Underneath the pierced footrest was room for a foot warmer that would be filled with embers from the earth.

Clockwise from bottom right: a plank highchair with a removable tray and pierced footrest, probably made by a Dutch immigrant; a mid-19th-century Windsor cradle; a circa 1900 pine piece; a circa 1833 painted pine cradle from Massachusetts with raised head and foot boards.

138

At Home with Country Furniture

adaptable furnishings that
suit a variety of decors

As the following pages show, most collectors of country furniture enjoy using their pieces and find them readily adaptable to the individual look of their homes. Some homeowners have chosen locally made antiques specifically to complement the regional character of their houses; others have used country furniture to create a period setting.

But no matter how they are used, most antiques are fragile and require gentle handling. Included in this chapter are recommendations for proper furniture care; you will also find advice on evaluating pieces that will be helpful if you are seriously interested in collecting. As one longtime enthusiast has found, collecting furniture can become a way of life. "It gets in your blood," she claims. "It becomes a hobby, a lifestyle, a pleasure, and a pastime. You make fine friendships collecting, you develop a heritage for your children, and it even helps keep you young in spirit."

An 18th-century four-poster is the centerpiece of a country bedroom.

Living History

For many collectors, living with antique country furniture goes hand in hand with an interest in America's past. "I love experiencing a part of our history," says one of the owners of this Texas house. "Owning old pieces helps us understand how little the early settlers had, and how much they made of it. Everything had a specific purpose; nothing was frivolous."

The couple prefer to put their antiques to daily use rather than display them as a museum would. In their keeping room, above, several

antiques give the large space a warm, comforta-ble feeling. Here a wooden easy chair, an Irish piece, and an 1830s Windsor rocker offer seat-ing near the hearth, and a late-18th-century Connecticut corner cupboard provides storage. Recalling a tradition of the colonial period— when one room served many purposes—the homeowners have also furnished the room with a maple Queen Anne folding bed, originally designed to save space in crowded quarters. Simple bed curtains hung on strings provide pri-vacy for overnight guests.

Furnishing their keeping room, left, with a Queen Anne folding bed—a predecessor of today's Murphy bed—allows the homeowners to use the room as a guest room. Made of maple and bearing its original red paint, the piece dates from around 1740.

141

New and Old

Although they were found in many early American households, upholstered furnishings from the 18th century are rare today; if they do exist, the pieces usually need re-covering. The recently restored 18th-century easy chair above showed traces of its original plaid covering; its new windowpane check upholstery recalls the old fabric. An alternative is a good reproduction covered in traditional fabric. The easy chairs and camelback sofa in the living room at left are faithful copies of Chippendale pieces.

To retain its original character, the owners of the antique country Chippendale chair above restored it using the original horsehair stuffing. The upholstery is new.

At left, reproduction upholstered pieces mix well with an 18th-century banister-back chair.

143

BUYING COUNTRY ANTIQUES

While buying antique country furniture can be an exhilarating and rewarding adventure, it is important to shop with care. Antiques are not always what they appear to be: some pieces are deliberately faked, and still others may have been repaired or altered unbeknownst to the seller.

Before you buy, educate your eye by looking at the best examples in books, museums, and shops. Learn to distinguish the lines and proportions of pieces from different periods. Once you start shopping, examine carefully under good light any piece you might want to buy.

Because new or substantial repairs generally reduce the value of an antique, it is wise to look for signs of recent work, such as nails, screws, and saw or plane marks that are not typical of the period in which the object is said to have been made. Run your hands over all surfaces, both finished and unfinished, to determine whether they feel the same; irregularities may mean replaced parts. Make sure any signs of wear appear in logical places—on chair stretchers and around drawer pulls, for instance. A piece that is worn in unexpected places, such as under a table top or inside a drawer, may have been altered or rebuilt. And check for inconsistencies in construction: if the dovetails on all the drawers in a chest do not match, the chest may actually be a "marriage" of parts from more than one piece.

Most sellers are honest, but potential buyers should protect themselves from those who are not by always asking for a bill of sale for all purchases made directly from a dealer. This receipt should contain a detailed description of the item, followed by the words "Guaranteed as is," and the dealer's signature. Most dealers are happy to furnish such a document.

Whenever possible, ask that the date of final sale be set for a few days later. Then, if you get your purchase home and find on further inspection that it is not what you thought it was—or what the dealer thought it was—you can return it. (Sales, however, are usually final at auctions, flea markets, and yard sales.)

If you shop at antiques fairs, which are generally busy, you may have little time to examine items thoroughly in the rush to buy. At most auctions, however, merchandise is displayed before the sale so that you can preview the pieces. Don't rush: inspect with care, but inspect only those items that really interest you and whose probable prices are within your budget. Then bid with caution. Do not trust any description of the sale items given by the auctioneer or the catalog; these sources are under no obligation to tell the truth.

Remember, not every genuine antique is necessarily valuable. In the past, as now, there were more mediocre craftsmen than skilled ones. Ultimately, you must decide if a piece meets your own aesthetic criteria. Fortunately, furniture that you are likely to find beautiful is also often the best in quality and value.

Painted Charm

The colorful painted decorations on the 1830s New England table and the circa 1825 Pennsylvania Windsor side chair above make them compatible with the collection of painted tinware displayed on the wall shelf overhead.

The owners of this home in a suburb of New York City chose 19th-century painted furniture to create a sophisticated yet whimsical decor. In the living room, right, a New England slant-top desk and a *faux marbre* storage box complement a folk-art menagerie that includes the large sturgeon decoy on the mantel, a turtle footstool, and a cast-iron giraffe floor lamp. In the dining room, above, the painted and smoke-grained table is appealing because, as one of the homeowners notes, it shows "somebody's imagination running wild."

The 19th-century furnishings at right were painted to create the illusion of wood grain or marble.

146

Versatile Wicker

Comfortable and adaptable, wicker furnishings have a timeless appeal that is well suited to almost any room. The owners of this house have created an airy, romantic decor for their sun porch with a mix of wicker in different styles. The ornate rocker at left is a Victorian piece, while the simpler rocker and matching love seat are in the Bar Harbor style, popular from around 1905 to 1925. The more tightly woven table and chair above are examples of Lloyd loom wicker, which was first available in 1917.

Contrasting bands of color and pattern like those on the matching Lloyd loom table and chair above are common on this type of wicker, which was machine-made from tightly woven paper.

Wicker accessories were prevalent in the Victorian era. Those at left include a plant stand, a lemonade caddy, and a small tray.

A FOLDING-CHAIR SLIPCOVER

Making a slipcover is an easy, inexpensive way to transform a simple folding chair into handsome seating. The directions opposite, for sizing and cutting your own paper pattern pieces and sewing the slipcover, can be used for any simple folding chair; the chair shown below is a standard type.

When making your patterns, be sure to use pieces of paper that are quite a bit larger than the part of the chair you are tracing, but not too large to handle easily. For the slipcover, choose a polished cotton or other fabric that has body and drapes well. When not in use, both the chair and the slipcover can be folded away.

MATERIALS

- 2½ yards 45-inch-wide polished cotton
- 2 yards 3-inch-wide grosgrain ribbon
- Thread
- Dressmaker pins
- Parchment paper or lightweight brown paper
- Masking tape
- Sharp pencil
- Yardstick

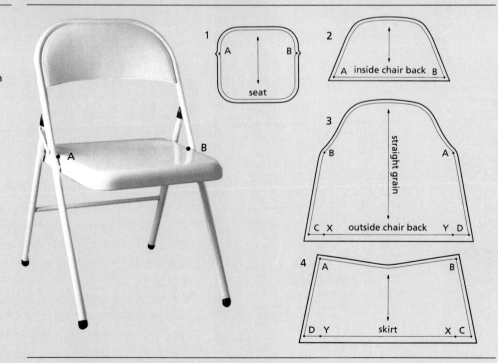

MAKING THE PATTERN

1. To make pattern for chair seat (Illustration 1), tape paper to seat. Trace outline of seat onto paper. Mark dots and letters A and B where front legs meet seat. Remove paper and flatten. At each dot, measure outward about ¾ inch and extend seat outline gradually to meet this point. Draw ⅝-inch seam allowance line around outline. Cut on outside line.

2. To make pattern for inside chair back (Illustration 2), tape paper around top of back, then push paper to back edge of seat; tape to seat. Continue taping around outside of chair back to where front legs meet seat. Mark dots and letters A and B where front legs meet seat. Trace from A to B around top of back. Remove paper and flatten. Draw straight line between A and B. Draw ⅝-inch seam allowance line around outline and cut on outside line.

3. To make pattern for outside chair back (Illustration 3), tape paper around top of back (paper should reach floor). Wrap paper loosely around back and sides and tape where front legs meet seat. Mark dots and letters A and B where front legs meet seat. Trace around top of back from A to B.

4. Measure from A to floor and mark a "Y" on paper; measure from B to floor and mark an "X." Remove paper and flatten. Draw a line between X and Y; extend line 2 inches beyond X and mark with letter C; extend line 2 inches beyond Y and mark with letter D. Continue outline from C to B and D to A. Draw ⅝-inch seam allowance line around sides and top from C to D. Draw 1¼-inch hem allowance line along bottom. Cut on outside line.

5. To make pattern for skirt (Illustration 4), tape paper around front of chair seat from front leg to front leg. Mark a dot and letters A and B where front legs meet seat. Continue as in Step 4 above.

◆

SEWING THE SLIPCOVER

1. Iron fabric. With fabric wrong side up, pin pattern pieces to fabric, being careful to align all pieces with straight grain. Mark all dots and letters on fabric. Cut out fabric; remove pattern pieces.

2. Cut ribbon in half. With right sides together and raw edges even, pin one end of each ribbon piece to fabric piece for inside chair back 2⅝ inches above points A and B. Machine-baste ¼ inch from raw edges; remove pins (Illustration 5).

3. With right sides together and raw edges even, pin back edge of fabric piece for seat to straight edge of fabric piece for inside chair back, matching dots A and B and easing fullness. Stitch ⅝-inch seam. Remove pins. Clip curves (Illustration 6). Press seam toward seat.

4. With right sides together and raw edges even, pin top edge of fabric piece for skirt to sides and front edge of seat between A and B. Stitch ⅝-inch seam. Remove pins. Clip curves (Illustration 7). Press seam toward seat.

5. With right sides together and raw edges even, pin fabric piece for outside chair back to inside chair back and skirt. Starting at D, stitch ⅝-inch seam, being careful not to catch seam allowances of inside back and skirt. Stitch to A, stop, and backstitch to reinforce. Continue stitching to B, stop, and backstitch to reinforce. Continue stitching to C. Remove pins. Clip curves (Illustration 8). Press seam to either side. Turn right side out.

6. Put slipcover on chair. Adjust length, remove slipcover, and trim hem evenly to 1¼ inches. Turn under 1¼ inch at hem to wrong side and iron; turn under ¼ inch at raw edge, pin, and stitch.

7. With slipcover on chair, tie ribbon in bow at back of chair. Adjust gathers; trim ribbon ends at angle, if desired.

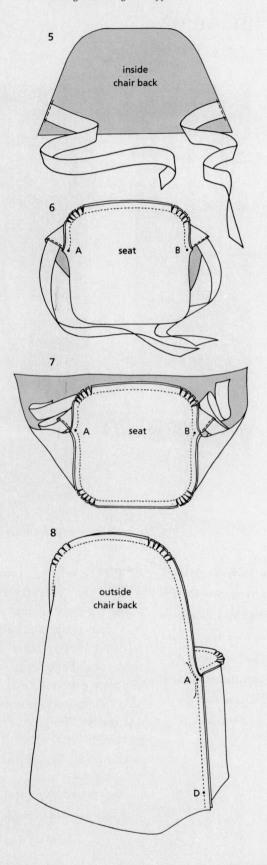

Shaker Refinement

Antique Shaker furnishings in the living room above include a rocker with a woven tape seat, a worktable, and a cherry tall case clock. All reveal how Shaker cabinetmakers reduced their design elements to essentials.

The owners of this New Jersey house began collecting 19th-century Shaker furniture several years ago because its pure lines made it compatible with their modern furniture. Today, their Shaker antiques fill every room and have long since replaced the contemporary pieces. "Shaker furniture is so beautifully made, it spoils you for anything else," says one owner. Their collection includes the maple worktable in the living room, above, and the ladder-back chairs in the bedroom, right.

The contemporary bed in the bedroom at right was designed to blend with the owners' Shaker antiques.

Purely Regional

The owner of this circa 1726 Huguenot-built house has gathered pieces for his keeping room, right, that reflect life in an 18th-century household. These include the burl bowl and the crockery on the hutch-table, and a Dutch brass utensil holder hanging by the fireplace.

The owner of this stone farmhouse in Ulster County, New York, is particularly interested in the history of the area, which was settled during the 17th and 18th centuries by the Huguenots.

Because his own house was built in the early 1700s by these French Protestants, he has made an effort to furnish it with regional pieces from about the same period. The large painted cabinet that dominates the keeping room, left and above, for example, is from nearby New Paltz. Made of yellow pine, the piece is rare because it retains its original "high feet," which allow for the storage of crocks underneath. Other furnishings include four banister-back chairs from the

Continued

The paint on the 1780s four-door yellow pine cupboard, above, has been worn down from years of constant use. The piece is unusual because it retains its original feet, which normally would have rotted away from age and exposure to damp floors.

The circa 1710 kas, or storage cupboard, above, probably once had a cornice that was removed to fit the piece under a low ceiling.

Albany area, signed with the maker's initials, and a small settle from Orange County, New York, distinguished by unusual "lollipop" arms.

Even before coming to America, the Huguenots had adopted many Dutch furniture-making customs, picked up during a period of exile in Holland. The 1710 gumwood linen cupboard above, with its original ball feet and butterfly hinges, shows this Dutch influence: still called by its Dutch name, *kas,* it is one of many such pieces made by Huguenots to be found throughout the area. Both the *kas* and the large burl bowl displayed on top of it came from the same house in New Paltz.

CARING FOR WOOD FURNITURE

While refinishing and repair of wood furniture is usually best left to a professional restorer, the general maintenance of your pieces can be done at home.

Among the most important considerations is taking good care of the finish on furniture, which is essential in protecting the wood against everyday wear and spills. Without attention, a finish will eventually dry out and deteriorate; veneers can buckle, old paint may disappear, and varnish may become cracked and dull.

In general, the best protection for furniture is paste wax, which is appropriate for any smooth finish, including paint, unless the surface is cracked or damaged in any way. If you have been using another furniture care product, such as a liquid or a spray oil, it is best to change to paste wax: you can safely use paste wax on any surface accustomed to an oil. Should there be an oil build-up on the piece, dissolve it first, using a soft cloth and mineral spirits.

For furniture that has regularly been treated with paste wax, you should not switch to a liquid or a spray oil; either can cause smearing and spoil the look of a surface.

If a piece has a thin, low-luster finish, called "close-to-the-wood" by some manufacturers, wax sparingly. Such a finish leaves the pores open to give the wood a more natural look; applying oil or too much wax can clog and whiten the pores, eventually spoiling the effect of the finish. When in doubt, use nothing.

Where it is practical, try to protect furniture from direct sunlight, which causes a bleaching effect. And avoid placing furniture close to radiators, warm air registers, and air conditioners; extremes in temperature can cause the wood to dry out.

It is also important to take care when rearranging furniture. If a piece is too heavy to lift clear of the floor, work a small carpet or a blanket under the feet and simply drag the piece along carefully. This will help prevent possible damage to the legs, which can catch against an uneven floorboard and weaken a joint. If you are moving a case piece, empty it and remove the drawers to lighten the load.

Spanish Colonial

T hirty years ago, the owners of this New Mexico hacienda discovered that their simple adobe house had originally been part of a complex of early-1700s Spanish colonial farm buildings long since fallen to ruin. The couple re-created the structures and furnished the rooms with period pieces that might have been owned by a colonial farmer of the region.

The guest room at right contains a ponderosa pine bed and a two-drawer chest that were both made in the Santa Fe area in the mid-19th century. Near the kitchen entrance, above, stands an 18th-century Spanish colonial grain-storage chest from the same region. Like most such pieces, the chest was joined with pegs, rather than with nails.

The owners of this restored 18th-century hacienda have furnished it exclusively with New Mexican

pieces, such as the 18th-century grain chest above and the bed and chest at right.

Colorful
Choices

The simple mid-19th-century country furnishings in this Ohio residence display
some of the many colors—including
warm reds and golds and vivid greens and
blues—that were often used in painting such
pieces. "Even barrels and buckets were painted

in the 19th century," says the homeowner.
"The makers tended to use any paint they had;
some of the most unusual and beautiful
shades came from mixing paints together willy-
nilly."

While the homeowner takes particular pleas-

ure in combining furnishings of different colors, she usually restricts her choice to three hues in any one room. In this way, she feels, each item can stand on its own and the effect is not overwhelming.

Among the pieces in the "taproom" above is a red-painted cupboard made from featheredged boards that bear traces of stenciling. The painted sugar firkins and barrel top that rest on the cupboard, and the carpenter's toolbox used as a centerpiece on the scrub-top farm table, complete the red, yellow, and blue color scheme.

Colorful antiques in the "taproom" at left include a scrub-top table—a mid-19th-century Ohio piece that retains its original paint—and an assortment of ladder-back chairs from the same period. The cupboard is made of featheredged boards that originally might have been used as wall paneling.

161

Well-Worn Patinas

During the 18th and 19th centuries, country furniture was often finished with paint because it preserved the wood and also disguised the fact that mismatched or inferior woods may have been used. Not only does original paint increase the value of an antique, but it also adds to its character. The owner of this house finds pieces like the farm table, left, and the corner cupboard, above, all the more appealing for their warm patina.

Traces of original paint appear on the 1700s pine step-back cupboard and the scrub-top table, left.

Well-worn furnishings, including a 19th-century corner cupboard, a country Chippendale worktable, and a child's arrow-back Windsor chair, bring color and charm to the keeping room corner, above.

THROUGH THE LOOKING GLASS

In early American homes a wall mirror—called a looking glass until well into the 19th century—was a supreme symbol of luxury. It was highly desirable, costly, and served few practical functions beyond the satisfaction of vanity.

From the 17th to the 19th centuries, the majority of looking glasses used in this country were imported from Europe. It is often difficult to determine the origin of a piece because similar woods were favored in this country and abroad. The same mirror styles were also popular on both sides of the Atlantic, but American versions tended to be less elaborate. Some of the simplest country mirrors were merely grain-painted frames fitted with glass.

The oldest looking glasses found in America generally date from the William and Mary period. These were usually made with square or rectangular frames topped with small crests.

As tastes in interior fashions changed, mirror designs changed too. The rather understated looking glasses of the William and Mary period gave way to more ornate ones that suited the tastes of the Queen Anne and Chippendale periods. These were typically embellished with gilding, cut-out fretwork, pendants, pediments, and crests ornamented with eagles, phoenixes, medallions, and baskets of flowers.

While the decoration varied, the shape of the glass was almost always square or rectangular until the 1770s, when oval Chippendale looking glasses appeared. The round mirror did not come into vogue until the early 19th century, when the influential English designer and cabinetmaker Thomas Sheraton popularized the round convex mirror. With its curving glass, the convex mirror could reflect a miniature panoramic view of an entire room.

Another product of the early 19th century was the "tabernacle mirror," so called because its architectural design bears a resemblance to Renaissance tabernacles. Unlike the convex mirror, these examples were rectangular in form and featured slender columns on each side. The columns, in turn, supported a cornice inset with gilded balls.

Most tabernacle mirrors were made with a smaller glass panel at the top that was usually decorated with painting and gilding on the reverse side. This type of work is called "églomisé." The term derives from *verre églomisé*, a form of painted glass with a foil backing that was popular in France and introduced to England in the late 1600s. Églomisé decoration on American mirrors was usually done with gilding rather than foil.

During the Victorian era, mirrors took on many exotic looks. Reflecting the current vogue for novelty, they were often shaped like ordinary objects such as keys or boots, and were made from unusual materials like animal horns or cigar boxes. Toward the end of the century, chip-carved "tramp art" mirrors made by itinerant craftsmen appeared.

Queen Anne looking glass with pierced and gilded shell decoration, c. 1725

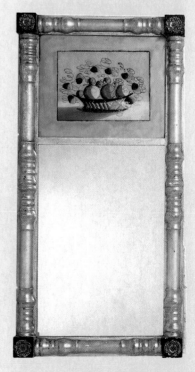

Gold-painted pine Sheraton mirror with "églomisé" decoration, c. 1830

Chippendale looking glass with a gilded phoenix in a fretwork crest, c. 1760

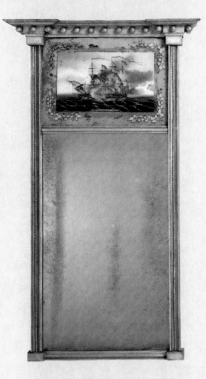

Tabernacle mirror with painting of U.S.S. *Constitution*, c. 1812

Grain-painted mirror decorated to resemble tiger maple, c. 1820

Folk-art mirror decorated with wood carvings, c. 1880

Simple Empire mirror with mahogany veneer frame, c. 1840

Early Victorian mirror with gilded gesso frame, c. 1840s

Two small Victorian novelty mirrors, c. 1890s

Chip-carved "tramp art" mirror, painted red and gold, c. 1900

Suitable Settings

In the 1830s Michigan farmhouse at right, simple 19th-century furnishings are set off by the marbleized diamond pattern on the floor, painted by the homeowners.

The country furnishings in these two rooms are particularly appropriate to their architectural surroundings. Although the owners of the 1830s Michigan farmhouse opposite began furnishing it with Victoriana, they eventually found that pieces made earlier in the century suited both them and the house better. "We kept going further back into the past as our knowledge and enthusiasm grew," says one of the owners.

The couple created a rustic look in their dining room with a collection of furniture from the early 1800s, including four Windsor chairs, a red-painted hutch-table, and a blue-painted Canadian sideboard. "We enjoy the warmth of the early pieces—the color, the worn paint exposing the wood, the feeling that they have

survived and been cherished, generation upon generation," comments the other owner.

In the parlor above, located in an old house perched on a riverbank near the Maine seacoast, the furnishings include a number of antiques the owner bought when he moved "down East." The two banister-back chairs are Maine pieces that date from the early 1700s; the tavern table between them, made around 1800, may also be from northern New England. Even the checkerboard on the table is locally crafted.

A marine historian, the owner also collects nautical memorabilia, such as the lighthouse painting over the fireplace. These days, however, he has started to limit his purchases. "The house and furniture go so well together, I like things just the way they are now," he says.

Regionally made pieces predominate in the Maine living room above. The circa 1800 pine and maple taproom table is from northern New England or Canada; the early-18th-century banister-back chairs were purchased locally.

Museum and Photography Credits

Cover: George Ross. **Frontispiece**: Kemble's, Norwich, OH. **Pages 8-11**: illustrations by Ray Skibinski. **Pages 12-15**: Wells-Thorn House, courtesy Historic Deerfield, Inc., Deerfield, MA/George Ross. **Pages 16-17**: Historic Deerfield, Inc., Deerfield, MA/George Ross. **Pages 18-21**: courtesy Museum of Early Southern Decorative Arts, Winston-Salem, NC/George Ross. **Pages 22-23**: Sayward-Wheeler House, York Harbor, ME, courtesy Society for the Preservation of New England Antiquities, Boston/George Ross. **Page 24**: Library of Congress. **Pages 26-27**: Towne House, courtesy Old Sturbridge Village, Sturbridge, MA/George Ross. **Pages 28-29**: Shandy Hall, Geneva, OH, courtesy Western Reserve Historical Society, Cleveland, OH/Jon Elliott. **Page 30**: George Ross. **Page 32**: (left) Society for the Preservation of Long Island Antiquities, Setauket, NY; (right) courtesy Henry Francis duPont Winterthur Museum, Wilmington, DE; **Page 33**: (left) Historic Deerfield, Inc./George Ross; (right) Western Reserve Historical Society/Jon Elliott. **Page 34**: (top left) Historic Deerfield, Inc./George Ross; (top right) Museum of Early Southern Decorative Arts/George Ross; (bottom) courtesy Jenkinstown Antiques, New Paltz, NY/George Ross. **Page 35**: (top left and bottom) Historic Deerfield, Inc./George Ross; (top right) Museum of Early Southern Decorative Arts/George Ross. **Pages 36-37**: (bottom row left) courtesy David A. Schorsch, Inc., NYC; (all others) Stephen Donelian. **Pages 38-39**: (left) Historic Deerfield, Inc./George Ross; (center) Western Reserve Historical Society/Jon Elliott; (right) Historic Deerfield, Inc./George Ross. **Page 40**: (left) Western Reserve Historical Society/Jon Elliott; (right) Historic Deerfield, Inc./George Ross. **Page 41**: (both) Western Reserve Historical Society/Jon Elliott. **Page 42**: (left) courtesy June Worrell Antiques, Houston, TX/Jon Elliott; (right) Historic Deerfield, Inc./George Ross. **Page 44**: (left) Museum of Early Southern Decora-

tive Arts/George Ross; (right) Historic Deerfield, Inc./George Ross. **Page 45**: courtesy June Worrell Antiques, Houston, TX/Jon Elliott. **Page 46**: (top) Museum of Early Southern Decorative Arts; (bottom) Historic Deerfield, Inc./George Ross. **Page 47**: (top) Museum of Early Southern Decorative Arts/George Ross; (bottom) Historic Deerfield, Inc./George Ross. **Pages 48-49**: (left to right) courtesy David A. Schorsch, Inc., NYC; collection of the Museum of American Folk Art, gift of Eva and Morris Feld Folk Art Acquisition Fund, NYC; Historic Deerfield, Inc./George Ross; Old Sturbridge Village; Robert W. Skinner, Inc., Boston. **Page 50**: (left and center) Chun Y. Lai; (right) Sayward-Wheeler House, York Harbor, ME, courtesy Society for the Preservation of New England Antiquities, Boston/George Ross. **Page 51**: (all) Historic Deerfield, Inc./George Ross. **Page 52**: (top) Christie, Manson & Woods International, Inc., NYC; (center) Museum of Early Southern Decorative Arts/George Ross; (bottom) George Ross. **Page 53**: Pocumtuck Valley Memorial Association, Deerfield, MA. **Pages 54-55**: Alan Shortall. **Page 56**: (left and top right) Historic Deerfield, Inc./George Ross; (bottom right) Society for the Preservation of New England Antiquities. **Page 57**: (left) George Ross; (right) Western Reserve Historical Society/Jon Elliott. **Page 58**: (top) Society for the Preservation of New England Antiquities; (bottom) Shelburne Museum, Shelburne, VT. **Page 59**: (left) Sayward-Wheeler House, York Harbor, ME/courtesy Society for the Preservation of New England Antiquites, Boston/George Ross; (right) Historic Deerfield, Inc./George Ross. **Page 60**: collection of the Museum of American Folk Art. **Page 61**: (top) George Ross; (bottom) Western Reserve Historical Society/Jon Elliott. **Page 62**: Western Reserve Historical Society/Jon Elliott. **Page 63**: courtesy June Worrell Antiques, Houston, TX/Jon Elliott. **Page 64**: (left) from the collections of the Henry Ford Museum & Greenfield Village, Dearborn, MI; (cen-

ter) collection of the Museum of American Folk Art, gift of Eva and Morris Feld Folk Art Acquisition Fund; (right) Society for the Preservation of Long Island Antiquities. **Page 65**: (left and center) Western Reserve Historical Society/Jon Elliott; (right) courtesy David A. Schorsch, Inc., NYC. **Page 66**: Hancock Shaker Village, Pittsfield, MA/George Ross. **Page 68**: Paul Rocheleau. **Page 69**: (top left) Metropolitan Museum of Art, NYC/Paul Rocheleau; (top right and bottom left) Hancock Shaker Village/Paul Rocheleau; (bottom right) Paul Rocheleau. **Pages 70-71**: (left) Western Reserve Historical Society/Jon Elliott; (center) Shaker Museum, Old Chatham, NY/Paul Rocheleau; (right) collection of the Museum of American Folk Art. **Pages 72-73**: Hancock Shaker Village/George Ross. **Page 74**: Philadelphia Museum of Art: Purchase. **Pages 75-76**: (all) courtesy Henry Francis duPont Winterthur Museum. **Page 77**: (left) Philadelphia Museum of Art, Clarence W. Brazer Collection; (right) Philadelphia Museum of Art, Gift of J. Stogdell Stokes. **Page 78**: from the collections of the Henry Ford Museum & Greenfield Village. **Page 79**: Philadelphia Museum of Art, Titus C. Geesey Collection. **Page 80**: (left) courtesy University Art Museum, University of Minnesota, Minneapolis; (right) Vesterheim, Norwegian-American Museum, Decorah, IA. **Page 81**: (top left) courtesy University Art Museum, University of Minnesota; (top right and bottom): Vesterheim, Norwegian-American Museum. **Page 82**: Neal Alford Company, Inc., New Orleans. **Page 83**: (both) New Orleans Museum of Art, Rosemonde E. and Emil Kuntz Collection. **Page 84**: collection of Mara Robinson, Sante Fe, NM/photo by Mary Peck, courtesy Museum of International Folk Art, a unit of the Museum of New Mexico, Sante Fe. **Page 85**: (both) collection of Mr. Theodoro Jeantet, Taos, NM/photo by Mary Peck, courtesy Museum of International Folk Art, a unit of the Museum of New Mexico. **Pages 86-87**: (all) collection of the Museum of

International Folk Art, a unit of the Museum of New Mexico. **Pages 88-89**: Alan Shortall. **Page 90**: designed by Ronald Bricke of Ronald Bricke & Associates, NYC, with thanks to Decorator Previews, NYC/George Ross. **Page 92**: courtesy The Corner House Antiques, Sheffield, MA/William Waldron. **Page 93**: (top left) courtesy The Corner House Antiques/William Waldron; (top right and bottom) collections of the Voigt House, Grand Rapids Public Museum, MI/Jon Elliott. **Page 94**: (both) courtesy Strong Museum, Rochester, NY. **Page 95**: (left) courtesy Strong Museum; (right) courtesy The Corner House Antiques, Sheffield, MA/William Waldron. **Page 96**: Stephen Donelian. **Page 97**: illustrations by Ray Skibinski. **Pages 98-99**: (far left) Chun Y. Lai, courtesy Strong Museum; (all others) courtesy Strong Museum. **Page 100**: (top) courtesy Strong Museum; (bottom) collections of the Grand Rapids Public Museum/Jon Elliott. **Page 101**: (left) collections of the Grand Rapids Public Museum/Jon Elliott; (right) courtesy Strong Museum. **Pages 102-103**: (all) Adirondack Museum, Warren M. Kay Collection, Blue Mountain Lake, NY/photos by Craig Gilborn. **Pages 104-105**: (all) courtesy Adirondack Museum, Blue Mountain Lake, NY/photos top row right and bottom row right by Richard J. Linke. **Page 106**: (both) collections of the Grand Rapids Public Museum/Jon Elliott. **Page 107**: (left) Witte Museum, San Antonio Museum Association, TX; (right) collections of the Grand Rapids Public Museum/Jon Elliott. **Page 108**: collections of the

Grand Rapids Public Museum/Jon Elliott. **Page 109**: (left) courtesy Strong Museum; (right) collections of the Grand Rapids Public Museum/Jon Elliott. **Page 110**: collections of the Grand Rapids Public Museum/Jon Elliott. **Page 111**: (left) Western Reserve Historical Society/Jon Elliott; (right) collections of the Grand Rapids Public Museum/Jon Elliott. **Pages 112-113**: (all) collections of the Grand Rapids Public Museum/Jon Elliott. **Page 114**: courtesy Jenkinstown Antiques, New Paltz, NY/George Ross. **Page 116**: (top left) Museum of Early Southern Decorative Arts/George Ross; (top right) Chun Y. Lai; (center) Western Reserve Historical Society/Jon Elliott; (bottom) Jon Elliott. **Page 117**: (top) Jon Elliott; (bottom) courtesy June Worrell Antiques, Houston, TX/Jon Elliott. **Pages 118-119**: (both top) Historic Deerfield, Inc./George Ross; (bottom left) from "Neat Pieces" catalog, published by the Atlanta Historical Society, photograph courtesy The Magazine *Antiques;* (bottom center) Historic Deerfield, Inc./George Ross; (bottom right) Stephen Donelian. **Page 120**: photo by Steven Mays. **Pages 120-121**: illustrations by Bill Meyerriecks. **Page 122**: (left) Chun Y. Lai; (right) Western Reserve Historical Society/Jon Elliott. **Page 123**: (all) Chun Y. Lai. **Page 124**: (left top) Chun Y. Lai; (left bottom) Museum of Early Southern Decorative Arts/George Ross; (right) Historic Deerfield, Inc./George Ross. **Page 125**: (left) Blue Ridge Institute, Ferrum College, Ferrum, VA.; (right) Chun Y. Lai. **Page 126**: Alan Shortall. **Page 127**: illustration by Ray Ski-

binski. **Page 128**: George Ross. **Page 129**: Witte Museum, the San Antonio Museum Association. **Pages 130-131**: (left and center) Historic Deerfield, Inc./George Ross; (right) Chun Y. Lai. **Pages 132-133**: (all) Philadelphia Museum of Art, Titus C. Geesey Collection. **Page 134**: Chun Y. Lai. **Page 135**: (left) collections of the Grand Rapids Public Museum/Jon Elliott; (right) Chun Y. Lai. **Page 136**: Western Reserve Historical Society/Jon Elliott. **Page 137**: (left top) Pocumtuck Valley Memorial Association/George Ross; (left center) collections of the Grand Rapids Public Museum/Jon Elliott; (left bottom) courtesy June Worrell Antiques, Houston, TX/Jon Elliott; (right) collection of the Grand Rapids Public Museum/Jon Elliott. **Page 138**: design by Madeline Armeson, Dennisport, MA/George Ross. **Pages 140-141**: antiques and interiors by June Worrell Antiques, Houston, TX/Jon Elliott. **Pages 142-143**: George Ross. **Page 143**: antiques and interiors by June Worrell Antiques, Houston, TX/Jon Elliott. **Pages 144-145**: George Ross. **Pages 146-147**: (both) George Ross. **Pages 148-149**: (both) courtesy The Corner House Antiques, Sheffield, MA/William Waldron. **Page 150**: (top photo): Alan Shortall; (bottom photo) Rob Whitcomb; (all illustrations) by Marilyn Rey. **Pages 152-153**: (both) Jon Elliott. **Pages 154-156**: (all) courtesy Jenkinstown Antiques/George Ross. **Pages 158-159**: (both) Robert Reck. **Pages 160-161**: George Ross. **Pages 162-163**: (both) Jon Elliott. **Pages 164-165**: (all) Alan Shortall. **Pages 166-167**: (both) George Ross.

Prop Credits

The Editors would like to thank the following for their courtesy in lending items for photography. Items not listed below are privately owned. **Pages 16-17**: consultant—Iona W. Lincoln, Curatorial Assis-

tant for Textiles, Historic Deerfield, Inc., Deerfield, MA. **Pages 36-37**: all Windsor chairs from the collection of Charles and Olenka Santore, except bottom row, left—courtesy David Schorsch, Inc., NYC.

Pages 54-55: grain-painted wooden cupboard created by Rubens Teles/Jay Johnson's America's Folk Heritage Gallery, NYC; unfinished wooden cupboard, "linen press" #9053—Mastercraft, S.J. Bailey &

Sons, Inc., Clarks Summit, PA; "Woodard Weave Checkerboard" cotton rug—Thos. K. Woodard, American Antiques & Quilts, NYC. **Pages 88-89**: painted arm chair—Jim Wagner/Zia Wholesale, Ranchos de Taos, NM, also available at American West, NYC; wood and twig folding screen—American West; armless bench, table, armoire, hand carved and painted snake—Origin, NYC; ladder, wooden bowl, Barbara Eigen peach and green pitchers, broom, tripod chair—Zona, NYC; Taos chair, simulated cow skull, Mexican pots—Adele Lewis, NYC; unglazed terra-cotta tiles—Country Floors, NYC; rugs and pillows—ABC International Rug Designs, NYC; terra-cotta plate with white decoration—Pottery Barn, NYC. **Pages 96-97**: wicker consultant—Arthur Napolitano, wicker repair and restoration, Hamilton Square, NJ; antique wicker furniture,

lamp, lace and linen pilows, frames—The Wicker Garden, NYC; Indian wool dhurrie rug—ABC International Design Rugs, NYC; vinyl wallcovering, "Woven Sprig," pale jade—Laura Ashley Home Furnishings, NYC. **Pages 126-127**: wallcovering, "Botanical Fruit"—Motif Designs, New Rochelle, NY; framed apple prints—Phyllis Wrynn/Park Slope Framing, Brooklyn, NY; "American Pitcher," white—The Hall China Company, East Liverpool, OH; hand-hooked rug—The Watermelon Patch, Manhasset, NY. **Page 150**: slipcovers made by Shirley Rosen, Philadelphia, PA; slipcover fabric, "Edwina" #EA-9580-F, table underskirt, "Mr. Darcy" #MD-9690-F, top cloth, "Cloverdale" #CLE-9570-F, all fabric 100% cotton, *Victoria Morland's Book of English Country Decoration*—Raintree Designs, NYC; sisal rug—ABC International Design

Rugs, NYC; "Primavera" limoges coffeepot, tray, cup and saucer, mini tureen, and sugar bowl, sterling silver teapot and napkin ring, lace-edged cotton napkin—Thaxton & Co., NYC. **Pages 164-165**: (top row, left to right) Queen Anne—Bernard & S. Dean Levy, Inc., NYC; Chippendale with phoenix—Bernard & S. Dean Levy, Inc.; tabernacle—Bernard & S. Dean Levy, Inc.; grain-painted—Eli Wilner & Company, Inc., NYC; (bottom row, left to right): Sheraton—Judith and James Milne/American Country Antiques, NYC; Empire—Judith and James Milne/American Country Antiques; oval—Eli Wilner & Company, Inc.; Victorian key and boot—Judith and James Milne/American Country Antiques; folk art—Cynthia Beneduce Antiques, NYC; tramp art—Kelter-Malce Antiques, NYC.

Index

Acknowledgments

Our thanks to Madeline Armeson, Judy and Alex Awrylo, H. Parrot Bacot at the Anglo-American Art Museum at Louisiana State University, Donna Barron at Old Sturbridge Village, Robert and Katharine Booth, Christian Carron at the Grand Rapids Public Museum, Conna Clark at the Philadelphia Museum of Art, Pauline Dowd at the Sayward-Wheeler House, Robin Farwell at the Museum of International Folk Art, Helaine and Burt Fendelman, Janey Fire at the Museum of American Folk Art, Carla Friedrich at the Museum of American Folk Art, Gretchen Fuller at the Strong Museum, Sally Gant at the Museum of Early Southern Decorative Arts, Beatrice Garvan at the Philadelphia Museum of Art, Peg Gure, Darrell Henning at Vesterheim/Norwegian-American Museum, Frank L. Horton at the Museum of Early Southern Decorative Arts, Joan and Jack Lee, Sandy Levy, Iona W. Lincoln at Historic Deerfield, Inc., Kenneth Martin, Adair Massey at the Atlanta Historical Society, Barbara Mauldin at the Museum of International Folk Art, Lee McGrogan at Western Reserve Historical Society, Tracey Meehan at the Adirondack Museum, Dr. Alan Minge and Shirley Minge, Dr. Marion Nelson at Vesterheim/Norwegian-American Museum, Barbara Randau, Charles Santore, Beatrice M. Snyder at Hancock Shaker Village, Kathleen Tetro, Joy Thomas, James Via at the Strong Museum, Kathy and Ken Wilson, June Worrell, and Dean Zimmerman at Western Reserve Historical Society.

First printing
Published simultaneously in Canada
School and library distribution by Silver Burdett Company,
Morristown, New Jersey

TIME-LIFE is a trademark of Time Incorporated U.S.A.

Production by Giga Communications, Inc.
Printed in U.S.A.

Library of Congress Cataloging-in-Publication Data

Country furniture.
p.cm. — (American country)
Includes index.
ISBN 0-8094-6766-6.   —   ISBN 0-8094-6767-4 (lib. bdg.)
1. Country Furniture—United States. I. Time-Life Books. II. Series.
NK2405.C68 1989
749.213—dc19   88-36821
CIP

American Country was created by Rebus, Inc., and published by Time-Life Books.

REBUS, INC.

Publisher: RODNEY FRIEDMAN • Editor: MARYA DALRYMPLE
Executive Editor: RACHEL D. CARLEY • Managing Editor: BRENDA SAVARD • Consulting Editor: CHARLES L. MEE, JR.
Associate Editor: SARA COLLINS MEDINA • Copy Editor: HELEN SCOTT-HARMAN
Writers: JUDITH CRESSY, ROSEMARY G. RENNICKE • Freelance Writers: JOE L. ROSSON, MARY SEARS, MICHAEL VARESE
Design Editors: NANCY MERNIT, CATHRYN SCHWING
Test Kitchen Director: GRACE YOUNG • Editor, The Country Letter: BONNIE J. SLOTNICK
Editorial Assistant: SANTHA CASSELL • Contributing Editors: ANNE MOFFAT, DEE SHAPIRO
Indexer: MARILYN FLAIG

Art Director: JUDITH HENRY • Associate Art Director: SARA REYNOLDS
Designers: AMY BERNIKER, TIMOTHY JEFFS
Photographer: STEVEN MAYS • Photo Editor: SUE ISRAEL
Photo Assistant: ROB WHITCOMB • Freelance Photographers: STEPHEN DONELIAN,
JON ELLIOTT, GEORGE ROSS, ALAN SHORTALL, WILLIAM WALDRON
Freelance Photo Stylist: VALORIE FISHER • Freelance Photo Research: PHOTOSEARCH

Special Consultant for this book: PHILIP ZEA
Series Consultants: BOB CAHN, HELAINE W. FENDELMAN, LINDA C. FRANKLIN, GLORIA GALE,
KATHLEEN EAGEN JOHNSON, JUNE SPRIGG, CLAIRE WHITCOMB

Time-Life Books Inc. is a wholly owned subsidiary of TIME INCORPORATED.

FOUNDER: HENRY R. LUCE 1898-1967

Editor-in-Chief: JASON McMANUS • Chairman and Chief Executive Officer: J. RICHARD MUNRO
President and Chief Operating Officer: N. J. NICHOLAS JR. • Editorial Director: RAY CAVE
Executive Vice President, Books: KELSO F. SUTTON • Vice President, Books: PAUL V. McLAUGHLIN

TIME-LIFE BOOKS INC.

Editor: GEORGE CONSTABLE • Executive Editor: ELLEN PHILLIPS
Director of Design: LOUIS KLEIN • Director of Editorial Resources: PHYLLIS K. WISE
Editorial Board: RUSSELL B. ADAMS JR., DALE M. BROWN, ROBERTA CONLAN, THOMAS H. FLAHERTY,
LEE HASSIG, DONIA ANN STEELE, ROSALIND STUBENBERG
Director of Photography and Research: JOHN CONRAD WEISER
Assistant Director of Editorial Resources: ELISE RITTER GIBSON

President: CHRISTOPHER T. LINEN • Chief Operating Officer: JOHN M. FAHEY JR.
Senior Vice Presidents: ROBERT M. DeSENA, JAMES L. MERCER, PAUL R. STEWART
Vice Presidents: STEPHEN L. BAIR, RALPH J. CUOMO, NEAL GOFF, STEPHEN L. GOLDSTEIN,
JUANITA T. JAMES, HALLETT JOHNSON III, CAROL KAPLAN, SUSAN J. MARUYAMA,
ROBERT H. SMITH, JOSEPH J. WARD
Director of Production Services: ROBERT J. PASSANTINO
Supervisor of Quality Control: JAMES KING

For information about any Time-Life book please call 1-800-621-7026, or write:
Reader Information, Time-Life Customer Service
P.O. Box C-32068, Richmond, Virginia 23261-2068

Time-Life Books Inc. offers a wide range of fine recordings, including a Rock 'n' Roll Era series.
For subscription information, call 1-800-621-7026, or write TIME-LIFE MUSIC,
P.O. Box C-32068, Richmond, Virginia 23261-2068.